Celtic Britain

Britain before the Conquest
An Archaeological History of the British Isles,
c. 1500 BC–AD 1066

General Editor: Andrew Wheatcroft

The Origins of Britain Lloyd and Jennifer Laing
Celtic Britain Lloyd Laing
The Coming of Rome John Wacher
Later Roman Britain Stephen Johnson
Anglo-Saxon England Lloyd and Jennifer Laing

Celtic Britain

Lloyd Laing

Charles Scribner's Sons

New York

Printed in Great Britain
Library of Congress Catalog Card Number LC 78–66127
ISBN 0-684 16225-3

Contents

Illustrations

Acknowledgments

The author and publishers would like to thank the following institutions and individuals for allowing photographs to be reproduced and for helping in finding suitable photographs: Aerofilms, Plates 20, 65; Ashmolean Museum, Oxford, Plates 4, 7a, 12, 15, 23, 49b, 49e, 56; The Trustees of the British Museum, Plates 1, 2, 3, 5, 6, 9, 10, 11, 14, 19, 33, 35, 36, 38, 41, 42, 50, 75, 87a, 93; the British Library, Plates 66, 105; Mr Peter Reynolds and Butser Ancient Farm Project, Plate 26; Prof. J. K. St Joseph and the Cambridge University Committee for Aerial Photography, Plates 21, 24; Carlisle Museum and Art Gallery, Plate 46; Colchester and Essex Museum, Plates 18, 47, 51, 52; Department of the Environment, Crown Copyright reserved, Plates 27, 28, 29, 31, 69, 70, 78, 80, 94, 98; Devizes Museum, Plates 16, 17; Gloucester City Museums, Plate 37; Kingston-upon-Hull Museums and Art Galleries, Plates 48, 54; the Manx Museum and National Trust, Plates 22, 83; Merseyside County Museums (Liverpool City Museums), Plate 39; the National Museum of Antiquities of Scotland, Plates 8, 34, 61, 63, 72, 73, 74, 77, 79, 86a, 86b, 86c, 87b, 90, 95, 96, 99, 100, 101, 102, 103, 104, 106, 107, 108; National Museum of Wales, Plates 40, 43, 44, 64, 68, 76, 81, 82, 89; Prof. P. A. Rahtz, Plates 57, 58; Reading Museum, Plate 88a; Scottish National Portrait Gallery, Plate 109; Sheffield Museum, Plate 88b; Winchester City Museum, Plate 55. The unattributed photos of coins (Plates 45, 49, 53) were taken from plaster casts of coins in the British Museum by the Liverpool University Joint Faculty Photographic Service, who also took Plate 91. All other unattributed photographs were taken by the author.

Introduction: Chapter one
The Celts in Europe

The story of the Celtic people is one of the most extra-ordinary in the history of Europe. Celtic traditions have endured despite the impact on European thought and custom of Goths, Huns, Vandals, Romans and several modern empires, yet at no time did the Celts have any sense of national identity. Today the term 'Celts' embraces many peoples with traditions as diverse as those to be found in Ireland, Wales, Cornwall and Brittany. The Celts have intermingled with most of the populations of western Europe to varying extents, and their legacy includes a host of famous place-names. The great rivers of northern and central Europe, the Rhine, the Danube, the Neckar, the Main, the Thames and many others owe their names to remote Celtic antiquity, and the names of cities such as London and Paris commemorate the presence there of otherwise forgotten Celts. From Celtic workshops have come some of the most magnificent treasures of early Europe – gold and bronze shaped into the vitally vigorous art that borrowed freely from Classical and eastern sources and which yet, like the Celts themselves, retained its peculiar brand of conservatism and individualism.

The Celts evolved at a time when written history existed only in the eastern Mediterranean and the Near East. Their culture evolved systadially with the development of iron technology in Europe, and their flourishing was the greatest achievement of the European Iron Age. Eclipsed by the civilization of Rome, they enjoyed a cultural renaissance after the Roman Empire collapsed that was to leave a legacy to the modern world. From their lavish art works to their humble hermits' cells perched on remote rock stacks off the Atlantic coast of Britain and Ireland, from their lyrical, mystical literature to their gruesome pagan religious observances, the Celts always were and remain a paradox.

Europe before the Celts
Until about the thirteenth century BC, European Bronze Age society had been remarkably static and conservative. European culture had gradually been improving its bronze- and gold-working, and developing warfare. Around 1200 BC,

1

however, a series of events interrupted the tempo of life in both the Mediterranean world and in mainland Europe. The original cause for the upheavals may have been an exodus of nomads from Russia, who stirred up hitherto static peoples. The Mediterranean teemed with sea-borne war-bands. For a while Egypt was taken over by barbarian rulers, and even as this happened the great Hittite Empire in Anatolia crashed. Mycenae, the hub of the great prehellenic civilization of Greece, tottered and descended into the Greek Dark Ages not much later, and wild Philistines overran Palestine. The collapse of the Hittite empire had wide repercussions, not least among which was the dissemination of the secrets of iron-working, which had for long been a Hittite monopoly.

Mainland Europe benefited in three ways from the Mediterranean's misfortune. First, the barbarians learned a new technology making beaten bronze work that could be fashioned into cups and shields. Second, barbarian Europe acquired a taste for wine, and opened the door to possibilities of trade with the Mediterranean whence came the intoxicating juice. Last, but not least, an interplay of ideas between the two areas led to the development of the heavy bronze sword; aggression could never be the same again.

The Bronze Age Europeans who chiefly benefited from these innovations were the immediate ancestors of the historical Celts. Archaeology knows them by the uncompromising name of the Urnfielders. They buried their dead in urns in flat cemeteries, and around 1200–700 BC they spread out from their eastern European homeland until their cultural influence was felt in France, Switzerland, Germany and even Italy. The Urnfield peoples probably spoke an early form of Celtic, and they developed many of the characteristics that were later to be associated with the Celts. They were the first builders of real hillforts in Europe (though types of forts had been known in the later Neolithic), and they were the first developed warrior society equipped with fine armour, weapons and shields. They were more successful farmers than their predecessors, perhaps because of the innovations of crop rotation, and their standard of living was higher than any previously seen in Europe. What they did not possess, that later Celtic societies exploited, was iron.

In later centuries the Greeks attributed the development of iron technology to two areas. The first was Anatolia, the land of the Hittites. The second region was a land at the edge of the known world, that of the Cimmerians, a little known people from the north of the Caucasus, whose ancestors may have included those who set the Mediterranean in ferment several centuries previously. It was the movement of these and other nomads into Europe around the eighth century BC that introduced iron-working into Urnfield lands.

The Cimmerians swept down into Europe, swarming over the Hungarian plain to the Swiss lakes, and possibly even as far as southern France and Belgium. From them the Urnfield people took up not only ferrous metallurgy but horsemanship as well. From 700 BC onwards characteristic burials can be recognized in Czechoslovakia and the upper Danube in which, typically, the dead were laid on four-wheeled wagons, set within timber mortuary houses. With them on occasion went the draught horses, which from the surviving bones can be seen to have been of Steppe pony type. Europe was gravid with the first great Celtic culture.

Hallstatt – the beginnings of Celtic Europe
The first stage of Celtic development is known as the *Hallstatt,* after a village in the Salzkammergut in Austria where an early cemetery connected with substantial salt mines is typical of its early flowering. Salt, as well as iron, was the currency in which the Hallstatt Celts calculated their wealth and power. Salt mining was not a new industry in central Europe. Places with names reflecting their importance as salt mines in earlier prehistoric times – Halle, Hallein, Hallstatt – were already being exploited before 1000 BC. By the seventh century BC there may have been as many as two dozen centres of salt production, which would have traded not only in the mineral but also in salted meat and fish. The preservative nature of salt has resulted in bodies of miners surviving from the Hallstatt mines, grisly reminders of the hardships of salt mining before the advent of modern technology.

Salt and iron provided the wealth, but farming still provided the basis of the Celtic economy. With the new metal tools, forests could be cleared quickly and crops harvested more efficiently. Farming became more productive, the population expanded, and for reasons not properly understood, aggression built up. A social pyramid, capped by chieftains and warriors, was maintained by farming and industry, and as fields were hacked out of the forest the Celts infiltrated new areas, determinedly reaching the English Channel and then crossing to Britain.

Meanwhile, as the Hallstatt chiefs grew prosperous on the proceeds of industry and improved farming, a new market offered exciting possibilities. The Greek world, emerging from its 'dark' centuries, was expanding its territories and establishing outposts on the far bounds of the Mediterranean. By the sixth century BC, Greeks from Phocaea on the Adriatic had set up a settlement at Massilia (Marseilles) in what was to become southern France, and here cultivated the first vineyards that Provence was to know. Thence a riverine trade route was pioneered along the Rhône to south-west Germany. By the sixth century BC the centre of Hallstatt power had thus moved from the upper Danube, upper Austria and Czechoslovakia, to the upper Rhine, south-west Germany, Switzerland and Burgundy, and these new areas soon began to benefit from the luxuries that the Greek traders had to offer. Richly painted Attic cups, bronze drinking vessels and the wine to fill them, were transported north to grace Celtic feasts in return for salt products, iron, and possibly slaves.

One of the beneficiaries of this enterprise was the so-called Princess of Vix, a lady of about thirty whose corpse was buried with all ceremony on a bier made out of the bodywork of a wagon (the wheels had been detached and set against the wall of the burial chamber), some time around the middle of the sixth century BC. Among her treasures were not only the familiar Greek cups and other drinking vessels but, more significantly, a huge bronze *krater* or mixing bowl for wine. This stands over 1.5 m high, and is without doubt one of the most distinguished treasures of archaic Greek art ever to survive. No such object has remained intact in its homeland. It was the art manifest in this and similarly exotic imports that stimulated the Celts into the creation of new and invigorating artistic expressions.

Under Greek and barbarian stimulus the arts of peace and war developed. Tools were improved and potters and metalworkers became more accomplished. Hillforts began to proliferate, and one notable example in southern Germany, known as the Heuneburg, was embellished with mud-brick bastions on stone foundations in imitation of the Greek, though no engine of war could ever have stood on their fighting platforms. Weapons and armour were con-tinually refined under stimulus from the Mediterranean.

In 540 BC trouble flared up. The Phocaean Greeks came into conflict with the Carthaginians, and fought for western Mediterranean supremacy in a sea battle at Alalia, off the coast of Italy. Since the Carthaginians won, and blockaded Greek trade, the standards afforded by Greek contact were temporarily lost. When trade relationships were re-established half a century later, major changes had affected the Celtic world. Once more the centre of power had altered, and a more advanced Celtic culture was evolving, centred on the middle Rhône and Marne.

La Tène – Celtic culture at its zenith

The new phase in Celtic culture is known in archaeological terminology as La Tène, and is named after a site on Lake Neuchâtel in Switzerland. La Tène (literally 'the shallows') was part of the lake deemed particularly appropriate to receive offerings thrown in by pious Celts to please the gods. These provided antiquaries with a range of Celtic objects unparalleled elsewhere in Europe when they were found in excavation in 1906–17. Finds included a mass of iron swords and other weapons, everyday ironwork, woodwork (including a complete wheel) and the remains of human skeletons.

The La Tène Celts are distinguishable by a change in burial rite. Instead of a rustic wagon burial, the élite were honoured by interment on a more elegant two-wheeled chariot, accompanied as before by weapons and armour and the requisites of an after-life feast. No influential strangers need be sought to explain the new burial rite; it reflects rather an increased achievement on the part of the La Tène warriors. Wagons are the vehicles of fighting farmers, chariots of fighters who are maintained by farms. The prototypes probably came from eastern Europe, but the Celtic chariots found in graves of the fifth century BC are distinctive, the outcome of skilled collaboration between carpenters, wheelwrights and blacksmiths, and they are in all ways superior to their nearest wheeled rivals in Europe.

Once again the supply of Mediterranean imports facilitated Celtic trade. This time the main routes crossed the Alps into central Europe and southwards into France. The imports came not from the Greek but the Italic world, for civilization too was developing and the focus moving inexorably towards first Etruria and then Rome.

The Celts in history

From the fifth century BC the La Tène Celts began to figure in the writings of Classical authors. They swagger across the last stages of European prehistory and into the first pages of history, flamboyant and brilliant. Their technology was for the most part equal to that of their civilized Greek and Roman contemporaries, and in some respects was its superior. Drunken, boastful and disorganized they may have been, but they were fearless and dynamic and the desire for territorial expansion was strong within them. Soon the La Tène Celts had extended their influence over the areas formerly occupied by their Urnfield and Hallstatt predecessors, and then they touched civilization itself. Hecataeus and Herodotos are two of the first writers to

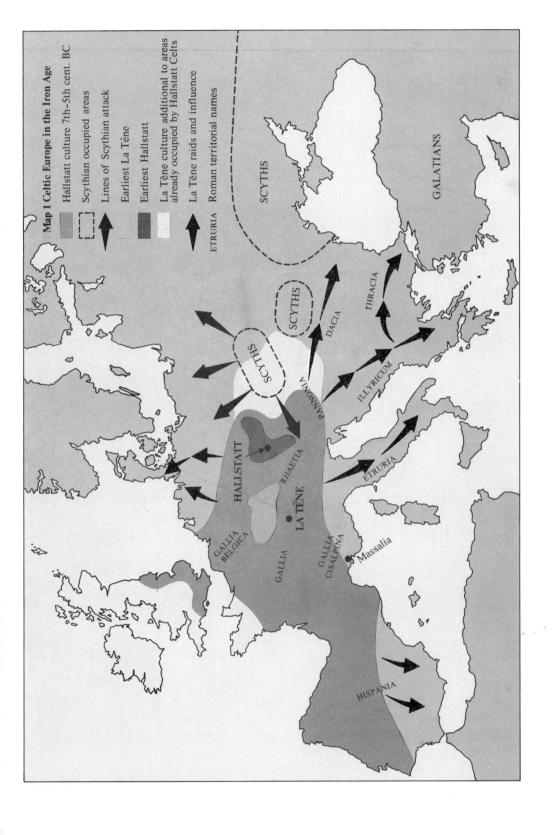

Map 1 Celtic Europe in the Iron Age

Hallstatt culture 7th–5th cent. BC

Scythian occupied areas

Lines of Scythian attack

Earliest La Tène

Earliest Hallstatt

La Tène culture additional to areas already occupied by Hallstatt Celts

La Tène raids and influence

ETRURIA Roman territorial names

SCYTHS

GALATIANS

SCYTHS

SCYTHS

SCYTHS

THRACIA

DACIA

ILLYRICUM

PANNONIA

HALLSTATT

RHAETIA

LA TÈNE

ETRURIA

GALLIA BELGICA

GALLIA

GALLIA CISALPINA

Massalia

HISPANIA

mention the Celts, and from this point on it is possible to chronicle Celtic expansion from the viewpoint of the Classical world as well as from archaeology.

The first civilized victims of Celtic expansion were the northern Etruscans in Italy, who in the fifth century BC witnessed their towns sacked by Celts from eastern France, Germany and Switzerland. Eager for plunder the barbarians streamed into the Po valley, and here they subsequently settled. For the first time Celtic peoples have historical names – *Insubres* settled around Milan, *Boii*, *Lingones* and *Senones* in Lombardy. Groups of Celtic warriors ventured even further south, to Apulia and the shores of Sicily.

In 387 the Roman legions were overcome by Celtic might at the battle of the Allia and Rome, which had been founded as a little Etruscan village in the sixth century BC, was sacked. Under the leadership of Brennus (one of the many Celtic leaders of this name mentioned by Classical writers) they rampaged in the Eternal City on a scale not to be witnessed again until the visitation of Alaric the Goth in the fifth century AD. The triumphant Brennus demanded his weight in gold, throwing his sword on to the scales on his side with the contemptuous words 'Vae Victis!' – 'Woe to the Defeated!' Brennus was out for loot, not for conquest, and left Rome to reorganize her defences, while the towns of southern Italy panicked in the face of the barbarian on-slaught. One Celtic chief was buried in Canusium (in Southern Italy), in a grave reserved for the local ruling family.

The Celts remained a force to be reckoned with in Italy until 295 BC, when the tables were turned and they were thoroughly beaten by the Romans. Gradually they were pushed further north until at last at the battle of Telamon in 225 BC the Roman army marched, triumphant, into northern Italy. By the time of the dictator Sulla in 82 BC northern Italy was established as the province of Cisalpine Gaul, and the long Celtic summer was at an end.

Italy was but one target for Celtic plundering. During the fourth century BC the Celts raided the Carpathians – Alexander the Great received envoys from the Celts of the Danube – and soon after, raids were reported in Bulgaria and Macedon. The Celts were unbeatable in the Balkans. In 279 BC they devastated Macedonia, which only half a century previously had been the hub of the greatest empire the ancient world had known, and under Akichorius and another Brennus penetrated Thessaly. At Thermopylae they met the Athenians just as the Persians had done over two centuries before. Their advance was not halted, and the warlike Volcae Tectosages pillaged Delphi, the sacred shrine of Apollo and the Pythoness. The booty was carried off and ended up in Toulouse.

These encounters with civilization gave impetus to Celtic opportunism with a new idea for profit – Celts now hired themselves out as mercenaries to any Hellenistic princeling who could afford their price. Celtic soldiers became commonplace in Greek armies. In 265 BC a division of Celts mutinied at Megara because the pay was unsatisfactory. King Nikomedes of Bythinia (now in Turkey) invited 20,000 Celts into Asia Minor, but the plan went awry, for these Celts imposed a rule of terror on the Greek cities. In 270 Celts were given territory near Ankara. This became the kingdom of Galatia (the name is the same as that of Gaul), which was to survive into Christian times. St Paul addressed a letter to the Galatians – in his time the inhabitants still spoke a recognizable Celtic as well as Greek. This has proved to be a lost kingdom, for, apart from a couple of brooches of Celtic type believed to have been found in Galatia that turned up in a Turkish antique shop, few remains of these Celts have been found.

Celtic terrorism in the eastern Mediterranean came to an end around 244 BC, when they were defeated first by Antigonas Gonatas in Macedon and then by Attalos of Pergamon in Turkey. Their fall is chronicled in one of the finest series of Hellenistic sculptures to have survived the ravages of time, the Pergamene Reliefs. Of these the most famous is the 'Dying Gaul' (actually a Galatian) now admired by visitors to the Capitoline Museum in Rome. The Pergamene school of sculpture is characterized by the first real attempts at naturalism, and subsequently led the Greek world in sculpture.

From the third century BC onwards the Celtic world began to shrink. In the second century Celts and Romans alike felt the scourge of another group of barbarians, Germans from north Jutland known as Cimbri, who joined forces with the Celtic Teutones and harried Celtic lands. Twice repulsed by the Romans, in 107 and 105 BC, they bore down on the Italian peninsula. In 102 the Roman general Marius defeated them, and an uneasy peace ensued.

During the first half of the first century BC the Romans began their implacable encroachment on Celtic realms. By 58 BC there had been a series of political crises in Gaul, arising from the collapse of old kingdoms and the emergence of new tribal groups. This time of upheaval provided Julius Caesar with the opportunity for the conquest of Gaul. Some Celtic tribes were prepared to ally with him, and with

their help he subdued the Helvetii (in what is now Switzerland) and pushed the Germans under Ariovistus back
across the Rhine. The Gallic tribes allied under the eminent
Vercingetorix, but were defeated at Avaricum and met with
little success at Gergovia. Vercingetorix was proclaimed
high chief of the Celtic tribes of Gaul at a huge assembly at
Bibracte (Mont Beauvray), then confronted Caesar in a last
desperate stand at Alesia. The battle was lost and Caesar
returned triumphant after eight years' campaigning to face
the jealousy that ended in bloodstained daggers in 49 BC.
By the time his adopted son Augustus was first Emperor of
Rome, Celtic Gaul had become four Roman provinces,
Narbonensis, Aquitania, Lugdunensis and Belgica. Roman
influence progressively made itself felt on the culture of Gaul
so that by the time the Empire collapsed Gaulish was only
spoken, as C. E. Stevens once pointed out, by witches,
occulists, and remote natives in the Eiffel. Beyond the
frontiers of Gaul, Celtic culture lingered on in central
Europe, but it was increasingly diluted by that of Rome.

Celtic Britain
While these events were all taking place in Europe Britain,
cut off by the Channel from the mainstream of Celtic
development, was evolving her own Celtic culture that outlived that of the Continent and indeed reached its pinnacle
when Gaul was already Romanized.

Celtic influence in Britain was heralded by trade and the
occasional isolated settlement of Hallstatt immigrants round
the coastal areas of England and Wales. While some may
have remained aloof from their culturally Bronze Age
neighbours, others were rapidly assimilated into the
population and modified the native culture with new ideas.
Novel styles of pottery and iron technology were among the
innovations. But the impact of the first immigrants on the
basic economy of Britain was slight – for most people life
went on much as it had done in centuries gone by.

The first Celts arrived perhaps as early as the seventh
century BC, bringing with them new designs of swords
which (like the other imports from Continental Europe)
were rapidly imitated by British smiths. Through the
ensuing centuries, particularly from the fifth century BC
onwards, trade brought an ever-increasing number of
Hallstatt and later La Tène imports that gave rise to British
imitations and modifications.

Only one colonization venture on any substantial scale
can be recognized from archaeological remains in Britain
before the late second century BC: a settlement of Celtic

warriors and their families from the Champagne, who established themselves in east Yorkshire. These incomers introduced the La Tène burial rite of inhumation accompanied by a two-wheeled vehicle in a rectangular ditched enclosure. The finds from the excavated burials all belong to at least second-generation families, but a date in the fourth century BC is likely for this minor settlement. Once established, the immigrants did their best to preserve some aspects of their native way of life, and still maintained their identity as late as the first century BC. But, like many newcomers, they also took on local traditions, such as native pottery styles, while the vehicles used for burial were travesties of the splendid chariots of their homeland – mere farm carts, the best that local technology could produce. The most famous cemetery is that at Arras, which takes its name from a deserted medieval village and farm of the same name near Market Weighton, in the southern Yorkshire Wolds. When excavated between 1815 and 1817, it comprised between 90 and 200 barrows. Although Arras has given its name to the 'Arras culture' as a whole, the cemetery excavated at Danes Graves north of Driffield was even larger – originally there may have been as many as 500 barrows, and about 200 were still visible in the late nineteenth century. At Garton Slack in 1971 an Arras-type chariot burial was excavated scientifically.

It is thus fairly clear that La Tène Celtic culture was well established throughout Britain by the first century BC and that local variations had grown up. It was at this point that a series of further Celtic invasions took place that have the distinction of being documented both historically and archaeologically. The newcomers were known to Caesar as the Belgae and they lived in that part of Gaul which lies just to the south of modern Belgium. Their arrival brought changes that on the one hand led to a great flowering of Celtic culture in the south, and on the other opened up trade links and contacts with Rome that eventually played no small part in the Roman conquest and the transformation of Celtic England and Wales into Roman Britannia. By this time, the first century BC, the names of tribes (Map 2) are known from history and from coin evidence, and the first British personalities people the history books.

It was the Belgae who brought a higher standard of living to the British aristocracy and whose influence led to the development of very advanced settlements, almost towns in the civilized sense. It was the Belgae whose patronage encouraged smiths and potters to greater achievements, and to whom we owe many of the finest pieces of art from

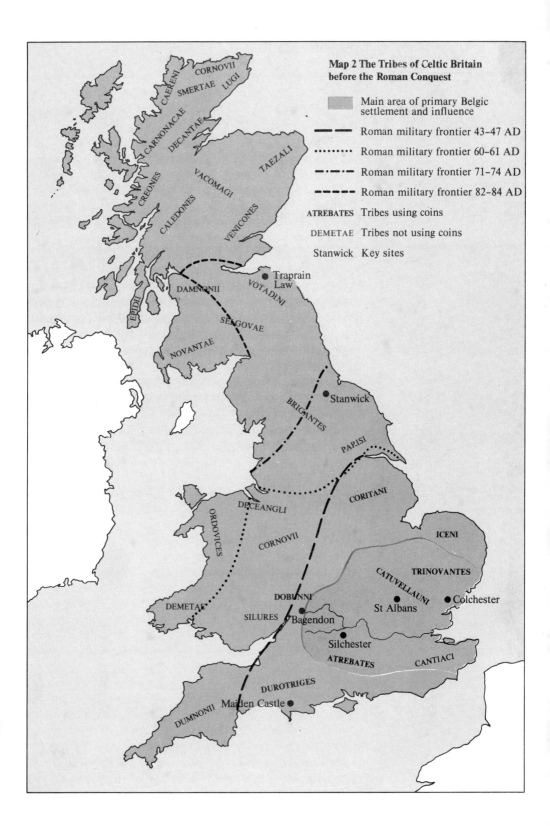

Map 2 The Tribes of Celtic Britain before the Roman Conquest

Main area of primary Belgic settlement and influence

Roman military frontier 43–47 AD

Roman military frontier 60–61 AD

Roman military frontier 71–74 AD

Roman military frontier 82–84 AD

ATREBATES Tribes using coins

DEMETAE Tribes not using coins

Stanwick Key sites

CORNOVII

CAERENI

SMERTAE

LUGI

CARNONACAE

DECANTAE

CREONES

VACOMAGI

TAEZALI

CALEDONES

VENICONES

EPIDII

DAMNONII

VOTADINI

Traprain Law

SELGOVAE

NOVANTAE

BRIGANTES

Stanwick

PARISI

DECEANGLI

CORITANI

ORDOVICES

CORNOVII

ICENI

CATUVELLAUNI

TRINOVANTES

DOBUNNI

St Albans

Colchester

DEMETAE

SILURES

Bagendon

Silchester

ATREBATES

CANTIACI

DUROTRIGES

DUMNONII

Maiden Castle

Iron Age Celtic Britain. This phase, the century and a half before the Roman conquest in AD 43, was in many ways the most glorious of all Celtic eras.

The British tribes in the south lacked cohesion and unity. Each tribe vied with its neighbours for territorial and political expansion. On the eve of Julius Caesar's campaigns to Britain in 55 and 54 BC, the tribes were squabbling amongst themselves. Then, in AD 43 the Atrebates sold out their Celtic ancestry to the Romans under the Emperor Claudius. Archaeology demonstrates it. Roman bases of Claudian date were built on their lands. Their leader Cogidubnus was rewarded with riches hitherto undreamed of in Britain, and unsurpassed until the Middle Ages or the Tudor period. Rome expanded rapidly: chariots and bold heroes were no match for legions and precision warfare.

By AD 47, England was held south of a line from the Humber to the Bristol Channel. By the 60s Wales had been overrun and by the end of the century most of what was later England and Wales had been effectively won for the next 300 years. The majority of Celts in these areas, always those regions most open to change and innovation (the very factor which had allowed the Celts their own influence in the seventh century BC), submitted and in the fullness of time took up Roman citizenship. Their story belongs to that of Roman Britain, for they were Romano-Britons not pure Celts.

It is, however, impossible to wipe out a millennium of cultural ties with a simple declaration of citizenship. Elements of Celtic life remained, even on the highest level of society. Some Roman ways were taken over – the pottery was copied, the metalwork changed, some aspects of religion persisted, for instance. Towns were built and the occupants of hillforts were moved into the Roman-style houses with separate eating, sleeping and bathing rooms. However the tribes were not usually fragmented, for the chief almost certainly held power over his subjects even if he had donned a toga and added '-us' to his given Celtic name. This factor might have had some significance in the ease with which Britannia coped with the withdrawal of military support in the early fifth century AD.

At this time the old province became increasingly open to further Continental influences, this time from pagan Germanic tribes. Where Roman ideas had permeated rapidly, Germanic ways of life took hold. For a time it is true, Roman ways remained in the south: sewers were kept clear, young Romans were sent over from the Continent to learn good Latin. But at the same time groups of Anglo-Saxons made their homes in the countryside and buried their dead with alien types of pottery. Almost certainly they began to trade, and certainly they influenced the local population. The evidence for this period despite modern archaeological and historical methods is still confusing, but the story of the cultural changeover in the fifth and sixth centuries is now 'dark' for only a few decades, not centuries.

Effectively, by the seventh century there is no doubt that the Celts were no longer a cultural entity in England. Those characteristics that can be traced from the fourth to the seventh centuries seem to be Roman rather than Celtic, though this may be due to the accident of preservation. The Romano-British population seems to have first mingled with, then fought against, and then been totally overshadowed by the Germanic tribes. The flamboyant Celtic culture that had started in the little salt-mining villages of Austria was at an end in seventh-century England.

Outside the Romanized areas, however, the Celts had fought first the Romans and then the Anglo-Saxons, and maintained their independence with such success that it is often impossible to distinguish whether a site in Scotland, or the remoter uplands of England and Wales, should be categorized in the Iron or the Dark Ages. Their cultural achievements were but a diluted travesty of the glory attained under the Belgae. Only in Ireland, outside the scope of this book, did the Dark Age Celts produce superb art and advance their culture.

From the fifth century the Celts were Christians. This factor has resulted in fewer remains being preserved, for Christian burials are characteristically free from material goods. The Dark Age Celts were neither civilized, nor were they true barbarians.

Chapter two **Iron Age Britain**

In 1886 Sir Arthur Evans, the future discoverer of the civilization of Minoan Crete, decided to carry out a small excavation with his father, Sir John Evans, on the site of an Iron Age cemetery at Aylesford in Kent.

The finds were not spectacular by many standards, but they opened up a new chapter in the understanding of Iron Age Britain. It is only a slight exaggeration to say that with one cut of the spade the Iron Age inhabitants of Britain were elevated from woad-painted savages cavorting through the pages of Caesar and other writers to dignified peoples with a well developed art and intellect worthy of further study. 'The Aylesford interments belong to an extensive Late-British cemetery of a kind not hitherto described by English archaeologists,' wrote Sir Arthur Evans in his report on the excavations in the 1890 volume of *Archaeologia*. 'The sudden appearance on British soil of this elegant exotic race of vases, in their pedestals and cordoned zones revealing still their pedigree of noble metal, and standing out, both in paste and contour, in strong contrast to the rude traditional urns evolved from basket-work and daub by our native potters, is a highly significant phenomenon. It can hardly be interpreted in any other way than as an indication that at the beginning of the period to which the Aylesford cemetery belongs, this Kentish site was occupied by an intrusive Gaulish tribe. The rapid diffusion of the same types of vessel throughout the south-eastern parts of England, as revealed by a series of kindred discoveries, seems to show that this invasion affected a considerable area.' With these sentences Evans introduced a new concept into British archaeology; that of archaeologically attested invasions from Continental lands in prehistory. Once established, this concept developed into the 'Invasion Hypothesis' which dominated archaeological thought in Britain for over half a century.

The Aylesford finds spoke not only of Continental immi-grants, but of far-flung trade links with Mediterranean lands, which before had been but dimly hinted at in ancient sources. But more than this, they illuminated a well developed warrior society. In the collection of finds – pots, imported Roman drinking vessels, brooches – one stands out. It is a bronze-covered wooden bucket, made in the last few decades of the first century BC and ultimately used to contain the ashes of a deceased hero. It was an object to be used and prized by a warrior, and its decoration depicted a fighting man. It does, in short, epitomize the basis of Celtic Iron Age society.

The handle of the bucket is attached to twin escutcheons in the shape of warriors' heads. They stare out across the centuries, the embodiment of pagan Celtic spirit, proud men with sharply chiselled features, jutting chins and determined mouths, each wearing an identical helmet from which sprouts an ornate crest which cascades down into two terminal spheres, recalling nothing so much as the feathered head-dress of an Aztec. The economy of the design is remarkable, but there is nothing crude about the heads. They are as accomplished as any produced by the best twentieth-century sculptors, and can take their place alongside works by Epstein, Hepworth or Giacometti.

The Aylesford escutcheons show one face of Celtic society at war. Another is to be seen on a companion bucket, perhaps of slightly later date, found at Marlborough in Wiltshire, at the beginning of the nineteenth century. Here, on a repoussé decorated bronze binding strip, is the profile of another warrior, his hair back-swept and perhaps lime-washed to make him look more fearsome, his luxuriant moustache curling round in the manner of an RAF officer of the Second World War. There can be no doubt that the bronze-smith intended him to look bold, but he has caught something else as well, absent in the Aylesford chiefs. Beneath the moustache the mouth has the hint of a smile, and the eyes betray something of the Celtic sense of fun. This chap would go down well with his repertoire of comic stories, retold round the cauldron at a Celtic feast.

Such human representations are all too rare in Celtic British art, but when they do occur they emphasize the human element in the world of Celtic Britain that is all too easy to forget amid the mounds of material culture that can merely be analysed and categorized. They reflect the antithesis and paradox, the maturity and childlike simplicity that was the essence of the Celtic peoples, and add depth to a picture which otherwise of necessity would have to be sketched in shades of grey.

Sources

Three chief sources of information provide clues to the world of the Iron Age Celts in Britain. Looking at all three is like turning on a television set with the sound turned down.

1 A helmeted Celtic warrior forms the escutcheon for this bucket handle from Aylesford, Kent, and embodies many qualities associated with the pagan Celts. It was found in a cemetery excavated by Sir Arthur Evans, future excavator of Minoan Crete, in 1890. Evans's discoveries at Aylesford led to a new understanding of Iron Age Britain. Height of head: *c.*4 cm

The people are there, the action is there, the colour is there, but we cannot be certain that our interpretation of the show is accurate.

The writings of the classical authors seem a promising source of information. These might at first seem to offer factual accounts of Celtic society but the Greek and Roman writers were not detached and scientific observers, nor did they always understand what they saw. Analytical commentary has only become possible with the development of anthropology in the twentieth century, and it would be naive indeed to suppose that modern anthropologists can believe everything that a society tells them about itself, or that the findings in one society can lead to useful inferences about another.

Greek and Roman writers, in no way inhibited by an ideal of scientific detachment, based their descriptions of barbarians less on how their subjects actually behaved than on how it was felt they ought to behave. The most famous 'Noble Savage' conjured up by J. J. Rousseau was simply an eighteenth-century shade tramping the path through Eden that was well-worn by earlier innocents in civilized thought. Man, conscious of his own inadequacies, has constantly sought an ideal world, a Golden Age before the Fall. As early as the eighth century BC the Greek poet Hesiod was seeking a mythical 'Golden Age' when all men were honourable, and in the Quest for the New World in the sixteenth and seventeenth centuries men sought to idealize the Amerindians just as the ancients had idealized the barbarians. The idealization of Pocahontas (d. 1617), the Red Indian princess who married an Englishman and died at Gravesend, is a good example – the popular version of how she saved the life of John Smith when he was captured by Powhatan is almost certainly apocryphal. The legacy is still with us, and perhaps unconsciously we seek an ideal world in outer space, the inhabitants of our globe having proved themselves incapable of forming a perfect society.

So, idealization of the barbarians was one red herring in the reports classical writers provide of Celtic society. It can be seen particularly in the speeches put in the mouths of barbarian chiefs by Classical historians, which contain noble sentiments intelligible to Classical readers but possibly meaningless to the audience the chiefs were supposedly addressing. The fine speech reported of the Gaulish leader Vercingetorix is a figment of Julius Caesar's imagination, a literary device to make the enemy seem more worthy of being conquered, and the conquest therefore more praiseworthy. Who wants to be known as the conqueror of a disordered rabble of yahoos in the backwoods?

The Classical writers were also, naturally, affected by the nature of the audience for which they were writing. Their readership was the urbane population of Rome and Athens, for whom barbarian customs would be interesting only if translated into terms they understood. Thus Celtic gods were equated with the nearest Greek or Roman equivalents, even though they might have only one minor attribute in common.

Another caution is the context of the descriptions that have survived. They are no more than thumb-nail sketches, background information simplified and compressed to set the scene for accounts of military campaigns or to provide the context for an anecdote. In the absence of the laws of copyright, authors copied one another or plagiarized other accounts, so that the modern reader cannot always be sure that a description really relates to the society it purports to describe.

Even so, Classical writers, particularly Caesar and Poseidonius, provide the fullest contemporaneous picture of Iron Age Celtic society that it is possible to obtain.

The second source of information to which we can turn is much more difficult to evaluate – the stories about the Celts set down by Christian monks centuries after the events. The source is not however completely worthless since oral tradition is tenacious – stories can be found repeated word for word even after the events described have become meaningless. Thus the poems of Homer ghost faithfully the world of Mycenaean Greece, which had passed away centuries before the poet was born, and thus the *Rigveda*, the great Hindu epic, was transmitted orally century after century, teacher to pupil, until it was finally set down in writing in the late eighteenth and early nineteenth centuries at the instigation of British scholars. If this seems hard to swallow, it should be recalled that as late as this century, an illiterate Hindu priest in Benares dictated a long religious poem, hitherto unknown, which in style and language was medieval, but which was not properly comprehensible to him. The sacred poem had been transmitted orally for many centuries, even after it had ceased to be properly meaningful to its narrators; to alter a word would have been sacrilegious.

The stories which survive from an Iron Age Celtic past are preserved in Irish and Welsh literature. The earliest versions are Hibernian, and date from around the ninth century AD, some 500 years or more after the events they seem to be describing. In setting them down, the monks have clearly misunderstood or failed to understand all the allusions, and Christian and other material has become intertwined in the narrative. In Wales the earliest surviving texts are even later, and correspondingly have been the subject of greater modification to make them compatible with the Christian faith. Even so, if the later additions are exfoliated by careful textual study, a collection of Iron Age images is left which corresponds remarkably with that provided by Classical writers. It must, however, always be remembered that it is highly unlikely that Celtic society was static, and even the oldest traditions relate to a state of affairs existing in Ireland in the first or second century AD, not necessarily to Britain in the first or second centuries BC.

Another important source is archaeology. This subject is notoriously unreliable when it comes to reconstructing a picture of how a given society functioned and thought, for ideas and deeds leave no tangible material traces. Pre-historic archaeological sources are, however, at their best on the technology and the economy of society, the very subjects on which written records have little to say. A further complication is the random natural selection of objects that survive. Iron and Dark Age people built mostly in timber and used leather, textiles and wood widely, so the more durable objects that do survive can be misleading. The relationship of what is found to what existed in any one period is variable.

The structure of society

With all these cautions in mind, what picture can be built up of the world of the pre-Christian Celts in Britain?

There is no doubt that Celtic society was based on tribes and the complex of social relations depended on the family unit as part of the larger tribal grouping. Certain kings or chiefs had ascendancy over lesser chiefs, depending on the politics of the time. At times takeovers and cultural influences were effected almost entirely from the top. This much is certain.

. The distribution of hillforts (within territories of similar proportions), the pages of Caesar, and, once they were introduced, the coins, corroborate it. Caesar stated quite clearly that the Celts were organized into *druides, equites* and *plebes* (learned men, warriors or nobles and the ordinary 'man-in-the-trackways'). He records at least one king, Divitiacus, who held lands on both sides of the Channel in the early first century BC, who clearly held more power than a mere tribal chief. In his wake came a procession of less shadowy historical figures such as Cunobelin and Tasci-ovanus. On the very lowest level of society were the slaves. Possibly, but not certainly, these unfortunates owed their existence to contacts with and ideological influences from the Romans. Caesar does not mention them, but he would not be expected to. Tacitus reported in the first century AD that one of the attractions of Britain was the number of slaves to be obtained, and it must not be assumed that these were merely those Britons the Romans managed to capture. In the first century AD at what is now Llyn Cerrig Bach in Anglesey, a votive hoard was thrown into a sacred mere.

When discovered in 1943 the offerings were found to include a slave-gang chain of iron with neck shackles so sturdy that it was used for pulling a tractor out of the mud before its true nature and age were detected.

The fullest picture of Celtic society, however, is given in early Irish writings which present a sometimes shocking, sometimes hilarious insight into the non-civilized way of life of the Celts.

For the Irish Iron Age Celts, it is clear that the family unit was large, not the nuclear group of father, mother and children, but the four generations of descendants from a common great-grandfather. This was known as the *derbfine* and had its own identity in law. Succession depended on it, and any member of a king's *derbfine* could succeed him: an uncle, brother or nephew would each be eligible. The *derbfine* owned land collectively and there was no individual ownership.

The larger group was the *tuath* or tribe, which was ruled over by its chief or king, and under whom were the nobles or warriors who estimated their wealth in numbers of cattle. Below the nobles were the ordinary freemen, who were essentially farmers who paid food-rent to the king and who received cattle from the nobles in return for obligations. At the bottom of the social pyramid were the slaves.

The learned men were a distinct class in society which lay beyond the regular bounds of the others. They were known collectively as the *aes dána*, the men of art. Their particular skills gave them status often above that of their birth, and in many ways they were respected as greatly as the warriors. The class was a motley collection including professional men, the lawyers, doctors, historians and musicians. Into it too went the druids, bards and seers and the craftsmen who forged iron and fashioned bronze. In Christian times the churchmen were fitted into the *aes dána*, but never comfortably, for it stemmed from another age in which the Christian faith had no place. Sometimes it seems, a warrior could also be a man of art. A warrior grave was found dating from the second century BC at Obermanzingen in southern Germany, furnished with sword, shield, spear and set of surgeon's instruments, including a probe, trephining saw and retractor, all of which would have been quite acceptable to his nineteenth-century counterpart. The example is Continental, but there is no reason to suppose that warrior-doctors were not also found in Britain.

Such a social structure is probably of great antiquity in Europe, and may stretch back into an Indo-European past in the Bronze Age or even Neolithic. It has its counterpart among the Germans, and later, in the world of the Anglo-Saxons. In more remote ages a similar system operated among the Sumerians. It was geared to family feuding and petty wars, to a world in which the concept of a state was irrelevant, and the only people who existed were those you knew or came into contact with in the course of war or trade. The tribal king was the government, and anything more abstract in concept would have been meaningless to the Celts. 'L'état c'est moi', said Louis XIV, as Vercingetorix or Cunobelin of the Catuvellauni might well have said before him. That is not to say the chief made laws, for that was the work of the jurists in early Ireland and no doubt of their equivalent in Iron Age Britain, though he could probably take the law into his own hands in matters of tribal importance. Everyday law was administered by assemblies, and blood-feud was an integral part of retribution.

A bizarre insight into the inauguration of kings and its close association with fertility rites is provided by the Welsh medieval writer Giraldus Cambrensis, writing about the inauguration of an Irish king in his own time: the source is his *Description of Ireland*. He relates how the people gathered together and a white mare was led in. The king elect then entered before the assembly, on hands and knees, and announced he was an animal. He pretended to copulate with her and she was then slaughtered and cooked. When the stew was ready, he climbed in the cauldron, bathed in the broth, ate the meat and drank what remained of his meaty bath water. After this, he was deemed to be king. The mare symbolized fertility, and by going through the ritual the king elect ensured not only his own regenerative powers, but those of his tribe and his tribe's stock. The rite has its echoes in the 'Corn King' rituals of other societies. This extravagant image of Celtic flamboyance is complemented by Classical writings describing the character of the Celts.

Diodorus Siculus, quoting from the Greek geographer Poseidonius, had this to say about the Celtic warriors on the Continent in the second century BC (quoted in *Early Celtic Art*, Arts Council, 1970):

> The Gauls are terrifying in appearance, with deep-sounding and very harsh voices . . . they wear a striking kind of clothing – tunics dyed and stained in various colours, and trousers, which they call *bracae,* and they wear striped cloaks . . . picked out with a variegated small check pattern. Their armour includes man-sized shields, decorated in individual fashion . . . on their heads they wear bronze helmets.

Celtic warfare, however, was as much a circus act intended to impress the enemy by its entertainment value as to terrify him with its savagery. Ordered battle lines were not a feature of Celtic military theory. Guerrilla tactics were the order of the day, the objective being to wear down the enemy by harrying. Nor did the Celts indulge in too much unnecessary bloodshed. If a champion could be found to take up their cause, so much the better, for thus were differences settled and a good entertainment viewed by all.

To judge from the descriptions of Classical writers, notably Caesar, the British Celts were every bit as good at putting on an act in the battlefield as were their Gaulish contemporaries. Caesar marvelled at their expertise as charioteers, little guessing that the gymnastics they engaged in were rehearsed battle feats, intended to impress their opponents into submission. His description evokes a picture of the Celt at war better than any that has come down to us (Caesar, *The Conquest of Gaul,* trans. S. A. Handford, Harmondsworth, 1951):

> In chariot fighting the Britons begin by driving all over the field hurling javelins, and generally the terror inspired by the horses and the noise of the wheels are sufficient to throw the opponents' ranks into disorder. Then, after making their way between the squadrons of their own cavalry, they jump down from the chariots and engage on foot. In the meantime their charioteers retire a short distance from the battle and place the chariots in such a position that their masters, if hard pressed by numbers, have an easy means of retreat to their own lines. Thus they combine the mobility of cavalry with the staying-power of infantry; and by daily training and practice they attain such proficiency that even on a steep incline they are able to control the horses at full gallop, and to check and turn them in a moment. They can run along the chariot pole, stand on the yoke, and get back into the chariot as quick as lightning.

The Irish epic, the *Táin Bó Cúalnge,* gives another picture – of the hero Cuchullain mounting his scythed battle chariot (translated by Joseph Dunn, *The Ancient Epic Tale Táin Bó Cúalnge,* London, 1914):

> Then took place the first twisting fit and rage of the royal hero Cuchullain, so that he made a terrible, many-shaped, wonderful, unheard-of thing of himself. His flesh trembled about him like a pole against the torrent or like a bulrush against the stream . . . he made a mad whirling-feat of his body inside his hide . . . he gulped down one eye into his head so that it would be hard work if a wild crane succeeded in drawing it out to the middle of his cheek from the rear of his skull. . . . The Lon Laith [Hero's Light] stood out on his forehead, so that it was as long and as thick as a warrior's whetstone, so that it was as long as his nose, till he got furious handling the shields, thrusting out the charioteer, destroying the hosts. . . . When now this contortion had been completed in Cuchullain then it was that the hero of

valour sprang into his scythed war chariot with its iron sickles, its thin blades, its hooks and hard spikes, with its hero's foreprongs, with its opening fixtures, with its stinging nails that were fastened to the poles and the thongs and bows and lines of the chariot, lacerating heads and bones and bodies, legs, necks and shoulders. It was then he delivered over his chariot the thunder feat of three hundred and the thunder feat of four hundred and he ceased at the thunder feat of five hundred. For he did not deem it too much that such a great number should fall by his hand at his first onset and first battle assault on four of the five grand provinces of Erin.

Thus does the Celtic warrior in his battle fury stand out larger than life, a swaggering braggart, his hand twitching for his sword, alert for insult, intended or accidental, through the swimming haze of alcohol that befuddled his mind. Classical writers marvelled at him, his fellows set him above all others and accorded him the hero's portion at their feasts.

Armour, apparel and weapons

But if this apparition is reached by historical sources, archaeology has furnished more tangible remains. Only one helmet has survived intact in England, but it is undoubtedly amongst the most splendid to have come out of prehistoric Europe. It was found at Waterloo Bridge, London, in 1868, and dates from the late first century BC. In keeping with other Celtic helmets, it consists of a conical cap made out of

2 Bronze helmet from the Thames at Waterloo Bridge, London. One of the best-known prehistoric British objects, it is also one of the very few Celtic helmets to have survived anywhere in Europe. Dating from the late first century BC, it may have been made not for war but to decorate a wooden statue. Height: 16 cm. Width between horns: 42.5 cm

two pieces of decorated sheet bronze, riveted together, with a third piece secured to the front. From the top spring two fearsome horns, with terminal knobs cast separately and added. Originally it was enamelled. Technically it is very accomplished, but as a practical protection against a heavy sword-blow its use seems very limited. Almost certainly it was a parade piece, not intended for real combat, and perhaps finally used to adorn a statue in a Thames-side shrine.

A companion to this impressive object, which makes its appearance adorning most ancient Britons in school history books, is another which is equally often used for the edification of the young, but which also probably never saw combat. This is the huge shield found in the Thames at Battersea. Like the helmet, it is made from thin sheets of bronze bound together and originally fastened to a leather or wooden backing. The front is covered with a rich array of ornament, arranged with careful symmetry which is particularly pleasing to modern eyes trained in the traditions of Classical art and which is probably due to Roman influence, for this fine object probably dates from the first century AD. At first sight the ornament, arranged in three roundels with central bosses, is purely abstract, but it rewards a closer inspection. The central roundel is joined to those flanking it with a design which, when viewed the right way up, becomes a creature with rivets for eyes, huge nose and flaring crest, reminiscent of that worn by the warriors on the Aylesford bucket. Turned upside down the same pattern takes on the shape of another face, with huge gaping mouth and outcurling whiskers. This 'comic-magazine' device of 'two faces in one' recurs in Celtic art, frequently in more obvious guises, and would seem to indicate a certain sense of fun.

An earlier parade shield and sword were thrown as offerings to a Celtic god in the River Witham in Lincolnshire. The Witham shield had a chequered career before it reached its watery resting place. Like its Battersea counterpart, it was made of sheets of bronze, originally on a wooden backing. On to this a spindly boar had been attached with rivets, and its outline can be traced on the surface of the bronze. In due course, however, the whole shield was dismantled, and a cast midrib was added, its central boss decorated with three glass studs. The original boar had been some kind of totem, designed to protect its owner. The new midrib, too, though less obviously totemic, had its creatures concealed in the ornament. A pair of bull heads join the central rib to the end roundels. The central rib is intricately fashioned from a

3 Bronze shield from the river Thames at Battersea, London. Another famous treasure of prehistoric Britain, it was found in 1857 and is 77.5 cm long. The symmetry of the ornament suggests Roman influence, and it was probably made early in the first century AD. The glass used to inlay this and the helmet in Plate 2 appears to have been imported from Italy or even the Near East

25

single piece of bronze, and the craftsman has foreshortened the whole design, so that the warrior carrying it would have seen it in proportion when peering over the rim of the shield – the long legs of the original boar may also have been to counter the foreshortening. It certainly must rank amongst the greatest masterpieces ever to survive from the Celtic past.

These pieces of parade armour are a physical reminder of the Celtic love of display. The Romans acquired the idea of military parade from the barbarians, and were in later times to fashion ornamental helmets with human vizors such as those found in the Roman fort at Newstead in Roxburghshire, or that from Ribchester in Lancashire.

The Witham sword is also a tribute to the smith's craft. Of its sheath all that remains is a gilt bronze mount, fashioned to lock on to the sword. It is decorated in repoussé work, embellished with fine engraving. Fragmentary though it is,

4 Scabbard mount, Standlake, Oxfordshire. Swords were an essential attribute of the Celtic warrior. This mount probably dates from the early second century BC, and was affixed to the top of a scabbard. It may have been made on the Continent, but more probably was the work of a British craftsman imitating Continental Waldalgesheim art. Width: 5 cm

it is a pertinent reminder that a warrior's sword was his most important possession.

The rich variety of swords and scabbards surviving from Iron Age Britain support this view. One of the earliest, from Standlake, Oxfordshire, was wrought in the third or second century BC. The original leather sheath has perished, but the iron sword and the bronze and iron mounts for the scabbard still survive. They are decorated with repoussé and engraved ornament, in a style reminiscent of the very best Continental work that characterized the finds from Waldalgesheim (p. 68). Of slightly later date, the sheath from Sutton on the River Trent in Lincolnshire also shows foreign influence, its closest models being Hungarian Celtic swords and some from Switzerland. The back plate is missing, but the front gradually tapers from a triangular mouth and is furnished with a central rib. Panels of ladder ornament and foliate and wave patterns are carefully incised on the bronze, which when the scabbard was first made would have caught the light in a particularly pleasing way.

One type of sword popular among the Celts is exemplified by a bronze-hilted find from North Grimston in east Yorkshire. Its warrior owner had also been buried with a second longer sword, rings from a sword belt, bindings from a shield, and bones from a joint of pork, to regale the

5 Sword or dagger hilt, probably from Yorkshire. This late second-century or early first-century BC hilt is in the form of a man with arms and legs outstretched to form the grip, and is typical of a series of 'anthropomorphic' swords found both in Britain and on the Continent. The blade is iron and the hilt is bronze. Note the backward-swept hair typical of Continental Celtic fashion from the fifth century BC onwards

hero at the after-life feast. The hilt of the short sword is fashioned into the figure of a man, his arms and legs out-stretched to form the grip. His head has long, back-combed hair, and he stares out balefully at the viewer. Such swords were widespread among the Celts – this example left the forge at the end of the second century BC.

British sword fashions closely followed those on the Continent. Almost as soon as the long sword of the Hallstatt Iron Age had been developed abroad, copies were being produced in Britain, from which native British forms evolved. In the fifth and sixth centuries daggers became popular among the Continental Celts, and this fashion spawned a series of British versions, manufactured primarily in the Thames valley, which were to last until the third century BC. At this time the La Tène Celts on the Continent were improving swords, and the new styles ousted the now old-fashioned daggers in Britain. The Thames valley daggers were the products of a highly developed market. They were geared to supplying the rich warriors of the fifth to fourth centuries BC with both the daggers themselves and their ornamented sheaths, and represent the first flowering of native British art. The earliest include some with simple openwork chapes (metal terminals of scabbards), and one made entirely from openwork which was found in the Thames at Hammersmith. The Hammersmith dagger chape was commissioned in the fourth century BC, and boasts a pleasing pattern of figure-of-eight motifs. Artistically it is not as accomplished as contemporary Continental openwork, but shows a great mastery of complex casting techniques. A solid sheath encased the dagger from Minster Ditch, near Oxford, and is embellished with a flowing pattern which almost comes up to Continental standards. It dates from the fourth or third century BC.

In addition to swords and daggers, the well-equipped Celtic British warriors carried spears. A particularly early example was found in the seventh-century BC hoard at Llyn Fawr, Glamorgan. Later but much more ornate is a spearhead from Datchet, on the Thames. It has a broad iron blade, to which are attached a pair of pleasing bronze mounts, decorated with curvilinear designs infilled with 'basketry' hatching, and dates from the end of the first century BC or beginning of the first century AD.

Archery was not an accomplishment of Celtic British warriors, but they made abundant use of slings. Slings have been, since the time of David and no doubt before, essentially a peasant weapon, and many of the slingstones found on Iron Age sites in Britain could have been the ammunition of a shepherd, intent on warding off wolves and other predators from his stock, as easily as the armaments of a warrior. However, the huge caches of slingstones from some forts, such as those amassed by the Durotriges in their last desperate attempt to defend Maiden Castle, were hardly collected for throwing at wolves, and fighting men in

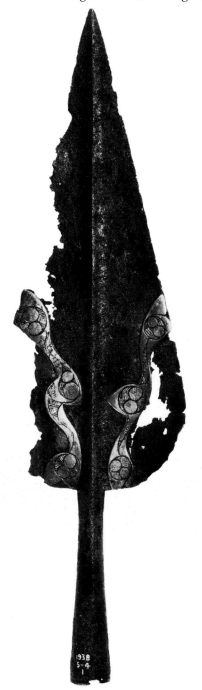

6 Spearhead of iron inlaid with bronze, from the river Thames at Datchet, Berkshire. The basketry pattern incised on the inlay is similar to that on mirrors produced in south-eastern England in the late first century BC (compare plates 37 and 38). Length: 30 cm

other societies have found the sling an effective weapon. Slingshot were usually just well-rounded pebbles collected from a nearby beach, but sometimes they were made of clay, as for instance at South Cadbury, Somerset.

The Celts as horsemen

It has already been noted that the Celts were fine charioteers, and although many warriors fought on foot, some went into battle mounted on sturdy ponies. Representations

7 Coins depicting Celtic horsemen. Although the coins are 'Roman' in style, the horsemen depicted are clearly Celts; (a) is a gold piece of Tasciovanus (c.20 BC–AD 10) and the reverse depicts a carnyx or war-trumpet being brandished. The obverse is a stylized version of a Greek head of Apollo, of which the wreath is the only element now discernible; (b) shows another horseman with a boar's-headed carnyx, of a slightly different type. Note in this and in (c) the use of reins. The obverse of this gold coin of Eppillus (c.AD 5–10) shows a winged figure of Victory, modelled on a Roman prototype; (c) is a gold coin of Verica (c.AD 10–40), and the horseman here carries a typically Celtic oval shield. The obverse type, a vine leaf, may allude to Mediterranean trade, perhaps in wine. From casts of coins in the British Museum (enlarged)

(a)

(b)

(c)

of Celtic British horsemen figure on some of the coins of the late first century BC–first century AD. The most interesting are to be found on coins of Tasciovanus of the Catuvellauni and Eppillus of the Atrebates, which show figures brandishing boar's-head trumpets, which seem to have served both as war trumpets and as a kind of totemic standard round which the warriors could rally. The mouthpiece of an actual boar's-head trumpet was found at Deskford, Banff, dating from the second century AD, but illustrating the kind of horn represented on the coins of Eppillus. A coin of Verica of the Atrebates shows a pony with a saddle cloth with four girth straps running from the corners through rings on the shoulders and haunches, from which are suspended decorative bands. The mane of the horse is braided. Several coins show that the Celts could guide the horses without reins, and a few show bareback riders.

Some steeds must have been very richly caparisoned. From Torrs, Kirkcudbright, has come a pony cap that was made in the second century BC. It was found in a peat bog and given to Sir Walter Scott. For long it was displayed surmounted by a pair of horns, but these are now suspected of being the mounts for drinking horns, and have been detached. Horns and pony cap are both decorated with attractive curvilinear ornament. Horse trappings of many different types survive from Celtic Britain. At the function of some we can only guess, but others seem to have been harness mounts, terrets (rings through which the reins passed on the yoke of a chariot), yoke mounts and lynch pins to fasten on the wheels. The finest are a series of richly enamelled mounts of the first century AD, the rich red of the enamel being set off by the deep glowing bronze background. The quality of the best is readily appreciable on the pair of mounts from Santon Downham, Norfolk, made around the time of the rebellion of Boudicca, where once again Roman-inspired symmetry makes the design particularly pleasing to modern eyes, or the comparable mount from the hoard found at Polden Hill, Somerset, along with a horse bit, terrets and harness brooches. Iron Age Celtic bits were of three-piece type, and numerous examples have survived, though mostly from the end of the period. One of the best, decorated with blue and red enamel, was found at Rise, near Hull in Yorkshire.

No chariot has survived from Iron Age Britain, though a wheel of what was probably a chariot was found in a Roman rubbish pit of the second century AD at Bar Hill, on the Antonine Wall. It shows admirably the skill of Celtic wheelwrights – the iron tyre was shrunk on, and the felloe was formed from a single piece of ash bent in a circle and fixed to a turned elm hub with lathe-turned willow spokes. From the remains of chariot fittings from Llyn Cerrig Bach, Anglesey, a chariot was reconstructed, and a life-size model made for a BBC TV schools broadcast. Open front and back, the small platform with wicker sides is just large enough for the charioteer and his warrior, the whole being pulled by two ponies in a double yoke. There is no evidence for horse collars in Europe before their introduction from

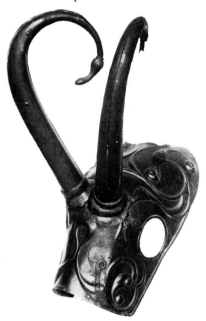

8 The Torrs pony cap, Kirkcudbright. Found some time before 1828 at Torrs Farm, Kelton, and owned by Sir Walter Scott and his family until 1921, this object is here shown with two 'horns' attached, which were found with it but which are not necessarily belonging to it – they may be either from drinking horns or from a lost helmet. The cap is one of the earliest native examples of Celtic art in Britain, and dates perhaps from the mid-second century BC. The holes were for the pony's ears. Total length: *c*.31 cm

China in the Middle Ages, and as ponies pull with their chest muscles, not with their shoulders, this form of harness designed originally for oxen must have been always rather unsatisfactory. The BBC experiment, however, showed it to be possible.

Personal adornments

A love of finery was not confined to Celtic warriors. Strabo, again quoting Poseidonius, said of the Celts (translation quoted in S. Piggot, *Early Celtic Art*, 1970):

> To the frankness and high-spiritedness of their temperament must be added the traits of childish boastfulness and love of decoration. They wear ornaments of gold, torcs on their necks, and bracelets on their arms and wrists, while people of high rank wear dyed garments besprinkled with gold.

Archaeology again bears this out. So ubiquitous as to be almost symbolic of the pre-Christian Celt, torcs – penannular neck rings often made, as the name suggests, from twisted metal – appear as finds or as representations in Celtic art throughout the Celtic world. The Dying Gaul of Pergamon wears one, so too does the moustachioed chief represented in the sculpture from Mseck Zehroviče in Czechoslovakia. The earliest torcs seem to have been worn by men and women alike; the finest of all, that from Waldalgesheim in Germany, came from a woman's grave of the fourth century BC. In later centuries, however, torcs were worn mainly by men, and may even have been the

insignia of the free-born male. The richest wore gold, the poorest made do with iron or bronze. Those torcs made of gold were flexible enough to be bent and sprung back round the neck of the wearer. In less flexible materials other means were devised to make them fit – one from Kelton, Kirkcudbright, has a movable section which pegs into the rest of the ring, a Continental device. Strabo reports that torcs were among the imports to Britain, and this may have been just such a trade article.

A series of outstanding gold and electrum torcs have been found in Britain, the finest of them from East Anglia. The most recent discovery was made at Ipswich, on 26 September 1968, on a building site. They were discovered by a digger-driver, who saw one sticking out of loose earth. When he tugged at it he found another hooked to it, and beyond that a further three, similarly intertwined. After washing them in the kitchen sink he realized from his experience as a scrap-metal merchant that they were gold,

9 Group of gold torcs or neck rings found at Ipswich in 1968 by a bulldozer driver. Torcs were the 'mark of status' of freeborn male Celts, and were made in a variety of metals. A great many gold torcs are known from East Anglia, and perhaps adorned the nobles of the Iceni, Boudicca's tribe. These are related to the Snettisham torcs, and date from the mid-first century BC. Maximum diameter: 20 cm

33

and took them to Ipswich Museum. Each of the five is made from a multi-faceted gold bar, bent back on itself, the ends joined to form a hoop. They were then twisted, and bent to form their penannular shape. Four had cast relief ornament on the terminals, the fifth was left plain. The hoard dates from the first century BC, and the torcs are similar to a fragmentary example from Sedgeford and another from North Creake, also in Norfolk. In all, thirty gold and electrum torcs have been found in East Anglia, amply

10 Gold torc from Needwood Forest, Staffordshire

bearing out Cassius Dio's assertion that Queen Boudicca of the Iceni when she rode into battle wore a 'great twisted golden necklace'. These were all almost certainly the property of rich Icenian chiefs and warriors.

The biggest single find was that made at Snettisham in Norfolk. Between 1948 and 1950 no less than 58 whole torcs and fragments were found in a spectacular series of hoards, and others have since come to light in 1964 and 1968. The Snettisham hoards comprise the richest array of Celtic treasures to come from British soil, and when they are set alongside the dearth of other Iron Age finds from East Anglia, they emphasize the contrast in the wealth of the nobility with that of the rest of the tribesmen who were notably impoverished. The finest Snettisham treasure is a heavy electrum torc, composed of eight strands each of eight wires twisted together, the ends being soldered into the sockets of hollow ring terminals, decorated with cast relief ornament in a similar style to that displayed on the Ipswich finds. A coin wedged in one of the terminals helps to provide a date for the series, which lies somewhere around 50 BC. In the same collection as the massive electrum torc was a gold bracelet, with a similar design in repoussé relief symmetrically arranged along a median line set within arcaded borders.

Outside East Anglia gold torcs are rare, but one found its way to Scotland, where its terminal turned up in a hoard of Continental Celtic coins at Netherurd, Peeblesshire. Another of simpler design with buffer terminals ornamented with a triskele pattern was found at Clevedon, Somerset, while a complete torc with twisted strands and ring ends was unearthed at Needwood Forest, Staffordshire.

11 The finest of the torcs from the hoard found at Snettisham, Norfolk. Made of electrum, it is about 20 cm in diameter, and came from one of a series of hoards found between 1948 and 1968. It was dated by associated coins to the mid-first century BC

Lesser mortals adorned themselves with bronze. An armlet in the form of a snake was found in a chieftain's burial at Snailwell, Cambridgeshire, buried around the time of the Claudian invasion, and there are a series of bronze collars of the first and second century AD of which that from Wraxhall, Somerset, is the most accomplished. The Wraxhall collar had a cunning fastening. It was cast in two pieces, held at the back with a ball-and-socket joint. The expanded terminals at the front conceal a tenon-and-mortice catch, and if these are pulled slightly apart, half the collar swings round on its joint to admit the neck.

If torcs and collars, armlets and bracelets were beyond the Iron Age purse, there were simpler pieces of jewellery. The most basic were safety-pin brooches and penannular brooches (like miniature torcs with sliding pins which could be pushed through woollen garments: the ring was then rotated to fasten the ends of the cloth together). Penannular brooches did not come into fashion until after the Belgic settlements, but thereafter remained the most popular type of brooch in Celtic Britain until the coming of the Vikings – they were elaborated into a bewildering variety of forms. Some of the simple Iron Age safety-pin brooches show the

Celtic love of ornament. On one series, best represented by an example from Birdlip, Gloucestershire, the bow was adorned with the addition of a bird's head. For the discerning there were safety-pin brooches in silver, exemplified by the pair of cloak brooches joined with a delicate chain, from Great Chesterford, Essex.

Classical authors frequently allude to Celtic tattoos, and the Dark Age Picts acquired their name ('painted men') from their addiction to the habit. There is no direct archaeological evidence for tattooing from Britain, but coins from the Channel Islands show tattoos on the cheeks of some figures and Caesar recorded tattoos on the British Celts. The hairstyles depicted on Celtic British coins show a variety of fashions and faces could evidently be clean-shaven, moustached or bearded. A series of tiny moustached bronze heads were found in the Welwyn burial of the mid-first century BC in Hertfordshire.

Farming

While the Celt as a warrior is undoubtedly the most colourful picture to come down for posterity, warfare was not a full-time occupation and the majority of Celtic people spent most of their time in rural agricultural pursuits, with a few taking up useful careers in the salt industry and other minority occupations; see Caesar's *Conquest of Gaul* (trans. S. A. Hanford, Harmondsworth, 1951):

> The population is exceedingly large, and the ground thickly studded with homesteads, closely resembling those of the Gauls, and the cattle very numerous. . . . There is timber of every kind, as in Gaul, except beech and fir. Hares, fowl and geese they think it unlawful to eat, but rear them for pleasure and amusement. The climate is more temperate than in Gaul, the cold being less severe. . . . Most of the tribes of the interior do not grow corn, but live on milk and meat and wear skins.

This account, reminiscent of an extract from *Gulliver's Travels*, comes from Julius Caesar's description of the British Celts. His comments about the climate might raise a few modern eyebrows, particularly since recent research suggests that the climate of Britain in Caesar's time was little different from that of today, but he can be forgiven for this pronouncement. Caesar was personally very fortunate in the weather when he visited Britain, for his account includes a description of how his soldiers raised a large cloud of dust when foraging for corn – earlier, however, his transports had been damaged by a particularly severe storm in the Channel, perhaps a freak thunderstorm caused by unusually fine weather?

Is the rest of his picture accurate? One thing is certain: Iron
Age Britain was a nation of farmers. An aeroplane caught up
in the kind of time slip beloved of science fiction writers
would have flown across a patchwork of small fields and
scattered round huts separated by areas of still dense forest.
Here and there on hilltops would be the ramparts of forts,
enclosing rows of buildings. It would have looked like this in
Caesar's time, and would have looked little different a thousand years earlier, though the hilltop settlements would
have had a slightly less defensive air, the forest would have
been that much denser and the climate too would have been
less wet and cold.

The climatic deterioration would have been felt more by
Caesar's 'tribes of the interior' who were the victims of the
rain-bearing winds from the west. In the highland north and
west, fields had to be abandoned towards the latter part of
the Bronze Age, reverting to pasture or waste ground and
many subsequently becoming covered with peat. In low-
lying areas, flooding caused settlements to be abandoned
and bogs and marshland to form.

However, there had been some changes in everyday life.
As on the Continent, the advent of iron axes from the
seventh century BC onwards meant that forest could be
cleared more readily, and this led to the rapid opening up of
large tracts of southern Britain hitherto but sparsely popu-
lated. Where centuries before trees had proliferated, golden
fields of corn waved under the sun and rain. Crops had
improved generally. At the end of the Bronze Age the
particularly hardy form of wheat called spelt was introduced, and a new, hardy type of barley (hulled instead of
naked) meant that for the first time a crop could be sown in
autumn and harvested before the spring-sown varieties.
The Greek writer Hecataeus noted as early as the sixth
century BC that the people in Britain reaped two harvests in
a single year, no minor revolution in the farming calendar.
Alongside the new grain crops were others, of lesser but not
negligible importance. One was the Celtic bean, which is
known from the lakeside villages of Somerset, others were
rye, club wheat and chess.

These innovations had several repercussions. To begin
with, the work load was spread and the harvest season was
extended, providing a fresh crop just when winter supplies
were running out. Second, the increased food production
meant a larger population could be sustained, and this no
doubt led to the boom which meant the landscape in
Caesar's time was 'thickly studded with homesteads'.

The so-called 'Celtic fields' are the most obvious

memorials in Britain to the industry of Celtic farmers. Not specifically Celtic, they span a long period from the end of the Bronze Age through to the end of the Roman occupation. The most characteristic are square or sub-square, ranging in size from ⅓ to 1½ acres in extent, and today they are a familiar part of the landscape of the chalk downlands. Calculations based on the fields at Overton Down, Wilts, suggest that the average field could be ploughed in a day, the type of plough used being an ard pulled by two oxen

12 So-called 'Celtic' fields at Fyfield Down, Wiltshire. Such small irregularly shaped fields were a feature of farming methods in Britain over a long period of time from the end of the Bronze Age until the end of the Roman occupation. They range in size from 0.82 ha to 3.7 ha in extent

travelling at about 2 m.p.h. The ard was a simple iron-shod type of plough, without a mould board to turn the furrow, and effectively it just scored rills in the soil. Traces of furrows found in excavation at Overton Down suggest that cross-ploughing was used to break up the soil sufficiently for sowing. Round the edges, where the plough was turned, the soil could be turned up using a wooden spade, and spade impressions were actually found in the Bronze Age fields at Gwithian, Cornwall.

Constant ploughing produced the lynchets which are a familiar feature of the lowland British landscape, but which are not peculiar to the Iron Age, belonging also to later periods. Lynchets were formed by constant ploughing on slopes which led to banks of soil forming at the lower end of the field and a hollow at the upper. Some lynchets served as field boundaries, though fields were also demarcated by land-cleared stones and (probably) hedges, fences or gullies.

Stock raising was, of course, also important to Iron Age farmers, not only in the highland areas but also in the south. Cattle was of the 'Celtic Shorthorn' variety, which first

appeared in Britain towards the end of the Bronze Age.
Sheep were a small breed, similar in many ways to the
modern Soay. Pigs were kept in small numbers and ponies
were bred, if only to pull wheeled vehicles such as the war
chariots that amazed Caesar on his arrival in Britain. Dogs,
as they are today, were kept as pets and worked as assistants
to shepherds and hunters.

Of course, farming had its hazards, and every now and
again the peace of the afternoon would be broken by a report

13   Philodendron, an Iron
Age type of pig, produced by
breeding a wild boar with a
domesticated sow. This
particular example was
photographed at Acton Scott
Farm Museum, Shropshire

of a marauding beast plundering the herd or crops. Wolf,
brown bear, lynx and wildcat would have all proved
formidable adversaries. Other creatures alien to Britain now
would have been fairly common in the Iron Age – beaver,
reindeer, wild ox, elk and pelican would have been seen in
some parts at least. Eagles and bustards must have been
fairly common.

Caesar's observation that it was unlawful to eat hares,
fowl and geese is supported by their frequent appearance in
Celtic religious art (particularly during the Roman period).
As recently as 1880 in north Wales it was considered an evil
omen to see geese on a lake at night, particularly on the first
Thursday of the lunar month, for they were believed to be
the attributes of witches. As for hares, Queen Boudicca of
the Iceni released one while praying to her goddess before
setting out on her anti-Roman campaigns, and hare legends
abound in later Celtic folklore.

Crops, once harvested with the reaping knives and sickles
that are known from a variety of sites, would have been
trundled back in wagons or pulled in sledges to the farm-
stead. Sledges were used in lowland Scotland even in this

39

century. At the farm, after the reaping, winnowing and drying, the grain would have been converted into flour or stored for future use. Burnt grains from numerous sites show that the parching of the cereal to make the husk easier to remove was not always without mishap. The corn was probably spread out on pre-heated stones to achieve this. The method of storage was in pits dug for the purpose, or in above-ground granaries, the floor being raised on stilts to counter rising damp or the privations of vermin. The storage pits were about 1.8 m deep, sometimes lined with wicker, as found at Worlebury, Somerset, or with stone, as on the Isle of Portland. Once filled, the pits would have been sealed with clay or marl. They were large Iron Age equivalents of food cans: once the pit was opened and air entered, mould would form on the sides and it could not be re-used until the sides had been cut back to a clean face. The above-ground granaries were probably used for seed corn, and were usually set well away from dwellings in case of fire. Grain was ground with rotary querns, which were an innovation of the Iron Age: hitherto grinding had been the laborious rubbing of one stone up and down on another in what is known as a saddle quern. One of the few examples of actual food being preserved was a carbonized loaf found at Glastonbury.

The daily round of the farm gave rise to all the subsidiary activities that are characteristic in every age. Milk would have been turned into butter and cheese, wool spun and woven into cloth. Looms are attested by the weights used for keeping the warp straight, and were of the upright variety. Round weights known as spindle whorls prove the use of the hand distaff for spinning. On the loom the weft was beaten down either with the long-handled bone combs which are common finds on Iron Age sites, or with pin beaters, consisting of a single bone pin set in a handle. These, and bone needles and awls, appear on Iron Age sites the length and breadth of Britain.

Some of the pits found in excavation were clay-lined and linked with gullies to the eaves drips of the roofs – these may have been used in the tanning of leather.

The farming calendar was broken up with festivals. Information comes from later Irish sources, but all the evidence points to their being of great antiquity. The most important was *Samain*, which was the Celtic New Year feast. Samain belonged to neither one year nor the next, and its celebration stemmed from the time when, with the exception of the few beasts that were kept through the winter for breeding in spring, stock was gathered together and slaughtered at the end of the grazing season. It was a fertility festival for man and beast and a time when the world was believed to be overrun with the forces of magic. Magical armies poured forth from caves and mounds, and mortals might pass into the other world. The festival was celebrated on the first of November and a dim shadow of it survives as Hallowe'en.

The next most important day in the year was *Beltane*, 1 May, which marked the date at which cattle were driven out into open grazing. Great fires were lit on this occasion, and cattle were driven between two large bonfires to protect them from disease, a ritual supervised by the druids.

Other festivals are recorded from later times, such as *Imbolc* on the first of February, which marked the beginning of the lactation of ewes, and *Lugnasad* on the first of August, which was in some way connected with the ripening of crops. Neither of these, however, need have been celebrated in Iron Age Britain, though they almost certainly had their equivalents.

Crafts and leisure pursuits

Many activities which are today specialist crafts were carried out in antiquity as home industries. Basket-making was one such, but apart from the impression of a basket on a pot from Dun Croc a Comhblach in North Uist and a basket fragment from Stanwick, Yorkshire, no archaeological evidence for baskets has survived. A related craft was hurdle-work, and very fine hurdles were found in the waterlogged conditions in the villages of Glastonbury and Meare in Somerset.

Glastonbury and Meare provide perhaps the clearest insight into the everyday life of Iron Age Britain. Although the two settlements have certain unique features, no others subsequently excavated have provided such a rounded picture of Iron Age activities.

In its own way the discovery of Glastonbury village was as curious as that of Mycenae or Troy by Schliemann. In 1888 a Somerset antiquary, Arthur Bulleid, happened to read one of the archaeological best-sellers of late Victorian England, Keller's *Lake Dwellings of Switzerland and other Parts of Europe*, which had been published just over twenty years previously and recorded the finds made in Neolithic lake villages round the edge of Lake Zürich revealed during a particularly dry summer. Bulleid was fired with enthusiasm, and set about looking for lake villages in his own country. Four years of searching terminated with the discovery of pieces of pottery in mole hills at Glastonbury in 1892. Five years of excavation followed, during which the nearby village of Meare came to light. Bulleid was assisted by H. St George Gray, who had been foreman under the greatest nineteenth-century excavator, General Pitt-Rivers. It was a fortunate partnership, for St George Gray was the best excavator of his age, and although the interpretation of the sites has since been questioned there is no doubt that had it not been for his skill much fascinating information would have been lost.

The Glastonbury village was almost totally excavated. The remains of ninety huts were uncovered, of which twenty or thirty were probably occupied at any one time. In its final stage it extended over a roughly triangular area, about 122 m by 91 m across, the huts being constructed of close-set vertical timbers with hurdles between. They were circular, with clay floors, and central clay hearths, sometimes attractively decorated with incised patterns. The doorways had thresholds and paved paths. The settlement stood on a shelf of peat and was enclosed by a palisade. Optimum occupation was reached in the first century BC, but may have begun as early as the third century BC with a group of small rectangular timber buildings, each about 3 m across.

The Meare village consisted of about a dozen houses, occupied in the third century BC, before the site was used first as a dump for refuse and then as the receptacle for hundreds of tons of clay.

The most interesting objects from Glastonbury and Meare were those of wood, since these have survived only rarely elsewhere. Numerous tubs and cups were found, either composed of staves or cut from the block. They included a tub with incised curvilinear ornament and a fragment of another with infilled hatching reminiscent of ornamental bronzework. Ladles, wheel hubs, wheel spokes, a ladder, a door, handles for knives, saws, awls, bill hooks and other implements, mallets, spade handles, stoppers and a variety of pieces of worked wooden beams and planks were all found. The expertise shown by the Iron Age carpenters was considerable. Tenon and mortice jointing was commonplace, and fragments of a carefully constructed frame may have been part of a loom. Dowels were used in some instances to fasten the staves of vessels together, though others were constructed like a barrel with hoops. The wealth of woodwork is a reminder how important this material must have been to the Iron Age Celts, and probably it was more widely used than pottery for domestic utensils. Indeed, the shape of many Iron Age pots recalls that of vessels made of wood, leather or even basketry, implying that pots were simply alternative imitations.

Antler was fashioned into a variety of tools also. It was employed in making handles, and particularly for the cheek pieces of bridles.

It was not all hard work at Glastonbury and Meare. Five dice were found on the site, as well as a dice box and various counters made from polished pebbles. Various games involving dice and counters seem to have been played in Iron Age Britain. The most interesting evidence for such Celtic amusements comes from a chieftain's burial of the late

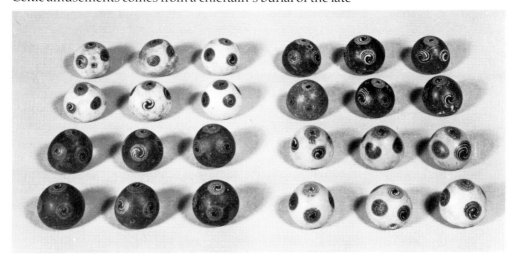

14 Set of glass gaming pieces from a chieftain's burial excavated at Welwyn Garden City, Herts, dating from the late first century BC. They were found associated with a much decayed board, and were probably used for a game akin to ludo

first century BC, excavated at Welwyn Garden City, in Hertfordshire. Here were not only found the playing pieces, but also the remains of what was probably the gaming board. Although the board itself had perished, it could be reconstructed from the metal mounts, which had served to reinforce it when it became battered from constant use. It would have been about 61 cm square and 4.5 cm thick, with a central iron boss which could have served, when inverted, as a cup. There were twenty-four glass playing pieces and it seems quite likely that they were used in a game not unlike ludo. Ludo, as we know it, was patented in the nineteenth century, but is much older and came to Victorian England by way of India. The Welwyn pieces are all similar, which suggests that at any rate it was some kind of racing game. No dice were found in the Welwyn grave, but a later grave at Stanfordbury, Bedfordshire, had one similar to those from Glastonbury. At Welwyn an alternative means may have been used for scoring throws: six fragments of beads and bracelets had clearly been put into the grave when already broken, and were therefore of little use as personal adornment. Experiments however showed that when thrown they would have come down in each case with one or two

43

sides uppermost, and thus could have been used for scoring. Dice were probably used in their own right for various games, of which the most likely involved throwing four up in the air to be caught on a blanket or cloth, the highest scorer winning.

Music certainly would have had its place at the Celtic feast, if not in the Celtic home. A bone flute was found in the Stanfordbury burial, and there are representations of musical instruments (apart from the carnyx trumpets) on Iron Age coins, though to what extent these were influenced by Roman coin designs is uncertain. Horns and pan pipes are depicted, and a horn of Iron Age date has been found in Ireland.

To return to more sober matters, a few other industries were carried out on a home basis. Braids were produced by tablet weaving, to provide ornamental borders for garments. The craft can be traced back to the Bronze Age in Europe and forwards into the Dark Ages. A group of triangular bone tablets for making braids was found in an Iron Age context at Wookey Hole, Somerset. Although much of the finer pottery was probably the work of specialist craftsmen supplying wider markets, coarse pottery was probably made at home. In some areas jet and shale working may also have been a home industry.

Metalworking

Of the many crafts practised in Iron Age Britain, that of the smith was pre-eminent. Smiths were highly respected members of Celtic society, they were men of art, possessed of skills which set them apart from lesser artisans, and which gave them a status in society surprisingly close to that of warriors. They produced goods for both the warrior and the farming markets. In the Irish epic cycle, the *Táin Bó Cualnge,* Culann the smith provided a feast for Conchobhar, king of Ulster, and the context of the story suggests there was nothing unusual about such an event. The smith god, Sucellos, was often equated with the divine warrior in early mythology, and Goibniu the divine smith of early Irish legends presided over the otherworld feast known as *Fled Goibniu.*

It is unlikely however that all smiths were equal in status. The master craftsmen who fashioned such masterpieces as the Snettisham torcs, the Witham and Battersea shields or the Desborough or Birdlip mirrors, must have been working under royal or noble patronage. Beneath them were lesser ranks, some at least itinerant, who set up their forges in fort or farm and repaired or made tools when and as they were needed. Their very mobility no doubt conferred certain privileges on them, and they could probably expect hospitality wherever their services were needed. Some may have been little better than tinkers, but even some of the more skilled craftsmen who could cast decorated horsegear in bronze seem to have been partly mobile, as the finds from the workshop on the farmstead at Gussage All Saints, Dorset, show. Here ornamental and other metalworking was carried out intermittently. Such men could hardly have

travelled light, for a considerably diversity of tools were needed to produce some of the more sophisticated metalwork, and as it would be inconvenient to prospect at each point of call for suitable ores it must be assumed they travelled equipped with a store of ingots and scrap metal.

15 Iron currency bars, shaped like the rough-outs for iron swords, from a hoard found at Salmonsbury, Gloucestershire, found in 1860. These doubled as currency and as ingots of iron. Average length: about 80 cm

The need for ingots probably explains the diversity of 'currency bars' that have been found in Iron Age Britain. Upwards of 1,500 of these have been unearthed, often in hoards. They vary in form, but the commonest are swordshaped, spit-shaped or plough-share shaped, of which the first two are the types most commonly found in hoards. That they were hoarded suggests that they had a value in their own right. A clue to their dual function as iron ingots and as currency is provided by Caesar who noted that iron ingots with a particular weight were used in Britain as a substitute for money. It is not impossible that people kept ingots ready for working into iron tools when the smith called. Ingots were probably produced in the first place by specialists working in regions where the ores were plentiful and whence they were traded.

Nothing is known about the processes involved in iron mining, and indeed iron may not have been used very widely for tools until as late as the third century BC. Caesar mentions the Weald as a major industrial area, and the rich collection of ironwork from the fort at Hunsbury suggests that Northamptonshire and Lincolnshire may have been another centre for open-cast mining. The Forest of Dean was exploited by the Romans, and the concentration of spit-type currency bars in the Cotswolds might suggest that Forest of Dean ironworking was already established prior to the arrival of Claudius. Smelting was done in shallow bowl furnaces, such as have been found at Kestor, Devon, where the surviving remains comprised a hollow about 30.5 cm diameter and 22.9 cm deep, filled with charcoal and slag. A more sophisticated furnace may have been used at All Cannings Cross, Wilts, where evidence suggested that a furnace with an outlet for tapping off the slag that accumulated at the bottom had been developed.

If the furnaces were simple, the products fashioned by the blacksmith's skill were not. Although the deliberate production of steel by the carburization of iron was not, as far as is known, a skill of Iron Age smiths, the qualities of accidentally carburized iron were apparently appreciated for edge tools. A tyre for a chariot wheel from the votive deposit at Llyn Cerrig Bach, Anglesey, was found to be of good steel and of a standard of craftsmanship not bettered until the industrial revolution: one modern smith said he would have been proud to have made it. Out of iron was fabricated a range of domestic tools that have changed little in design over the centuries – hammers, knives, gouges, chisels, saws, axes, reaping hooks, sickles, shears, adzes, horse-bits, swords, daggers, ferrules and a variety of other smaller objects along with sophisticated wrought-iron fire-dogs and cauldron chains.

The growth of ironworking led to a lessening need for bronze, though it still remained the main material for ornamental work. It was cast in one-piece clay moulds using the *cire-perdue* method, whereby a wax model was cased in clay before the wax was melted and allowed to run out. The technique is well demonstrated from finds at Gussage All Saints (Dorset). This site produced over 8,000 fragments of moulds for casting bridle-bit links, terrets (rings for reins to pass through), lynch-pins (for chariots and other wheeled vehicles) and strap unions. In addition there were fragments of crucibles, iron and bronze fragments and implements, part of a horse-bit, bone tools, a copper billet or small ingot, slag and bits of furnace clay. The metalworking was dated to the second or first century BC by radiocarbon, and is particularly interesting in view of the fact that the site on which it took place was seemingly a relatively minor farm-stead at which the foundry had been set up for a brief but intensive period.

The same process of casting was used for other metals, such as silver and gold. Recent studies of engraving with scribers, gravers, scorpers and tracers show that Iron Age smiths had a subtle appreciation of the use of different types of engraved line for different reflecting surfaces. The castings at Gussage All Saints suggest that the uses of various surface finishes were also appreciated; the rougher surfaces on some of the torcs found at Ipswich, Suffolk, in 1968–70 were perhaps left deliberately to produce a glitter rather than a glint when caught by the light.

As yet few manufacturing sites have been discovered. Apart from Gussage, the only foundry engaged in the production of ornamental metalwork that has been excavated was that at South Cadbury, Somerset. Here an ornamental shield boss and some other scrap metal had been collected near a group of furnaces adjacent to which were scattered metalworking tools such as punches, tracers and scribers of bronze and iron.

There are a few instances of metalworking on a minor industrial scale. Certain types of safety-pin brooches made in Wessex seem to have been the product of a single centre somewhere near Salisbury in the fourth or third centuries BC – all have been found within a 55-km radius. Specialist 'factories' also existed to supply the élite. The fine gold torcs discussed on pp. 33–5 were the product of one workshop, and from the third century BC several regional schools with their own characteristics were producing swords.

A few other industries seem to have been run on a commercial basis. Of these the most important was salt production. The main source was sea-water which was run into large evaporation pans round the south-east coast of Britain. The crude salt left after the heat of summer, along with the salt-rich underlying clay of the pan lining, was then made into a saline solution which could be boiled in pans – at Ingoldmells (Lincs) these were pre-formed to produce rectangular bars of salt-cake. In other cases the salt was 'cast' in clay moulds, and various types of salt container and moulds are known, notably from Purbeck, Dorset. This salt industry seems to have been established in Britain as early as the fifth century BC.

A minor industry, but one nevertheless operated on a commercial scale, was the production of Kimmeridge shale – this was boosted in the first century BC by the introduction of the pole-lathe. It was a type of oily, dark-brown shale found in the vicinity of the Isle of Purbeck, and was fabricated into bracelets, armlets, anklets and pendants. The trade was concentrated in a 74-km radius of the centre of production (though some products went further afield), and continued into the Roman period.

Pottery

Pottery too in certain cases seems to have been produced for more than local markets. Some early bowls coated with

16 Group of pots from the farmstead at All Cannings Cross, Wiltshire. They consist of a situlate urn with finger-nail ornament on shoulder and rim, and two bowls decorated with haematite in order to imitate bronze – a bronze vessel very similar in shape to that on the right was found in a late Bronze Age hoard at Welby, Leicestershire. These vessels are typical of what used to be termed 'Early Iron Age A', and the urn on the left clearly betrays its late Bronze Age ancestry. The smallest pot is about 13 cm high

haematite (iron oxide) to imitate bronze, that are found in Wessex, are so similar that they must surely have been the products of one centre; later in the Iron Age decorated pots made in Cornwall were being traded to Devon, Somerset and Hampshire. In the Welsh Marches and Gloucestershire other types of pottery were produced in at least four centres to supply settlements up to 148 km away.

Iron Age pottery is in general not without charm. At its best it displays clean lines and elegant profiles. The early Wessex haematite-coated bowls have an attractive simplicity, while the pots produced in the south-west by commercial potters, best known from the finds from Glastonbury and Meare, delight the eye with their rich curvilinear incised ornament in a style inspired by contemporary work in Brittany. The swelling shoulders are adorned with geometric and scroll patterns, with swags, running scrolls, lozenges and other patterns infilled with hatching to emphasize their lines. Similar ornament is to be found on pleasingly rounded bowls of the first centuries BC and AD, which have been unearthed in the central Thames area and northwards into Northamptonshire. Here swags were favoured, though zones of hatched lozenges and running scrolls do occur, notably on the pots from Hunsbury, Northants. Simpler linear ornament is widespread in space and time, and enlivens the burnished surfaces of hand-made vessels, occasionally relieved with impressed dots or simple curving patterns in arches or swags.

Zig-zags and pendant triangles festoon some of the earliest pots from Iron Age Britain – those made in the

17 Large urn from All Cannings Cross. This, and other early pottery from All Cannings Cross (see Plate 16) shows features of Continental 'Urnfield' wares of eastern France and western Germany, though they do not necessarily imply immigrants. Probably seventh century BC

eighth–seventh century BC. The pottery was used at sites such as All Cannings Cross in Wiltshire, which was occupied during the end of the Bronze Age and the beginning of the Iron. Intermittently, cordons appear to relieve the smooth lines of the vessels and were eventually employed along with comb patterns and corrugations on the pottery of the Belgae.

Although ornamentally less interesting, in terms of simple design Belgic pottery is superb. Produced on the wheel for the first time, it is thin-walled and often burnished to a pleasing black shine. Of particular elegance are the tall pedestal urns, with cordoned shoulders, and the small cordoned bead-rim bowls. Charming too are the vessels archaeologists enigmatically call *tazzas*, with tall pedestal bases surmounted by cordoned bowls, which look very much like art deco fruit bowls. Towards the end of the Iron Age new forms of vessels inspired by Gallo-Roman models gained great popularity in southern Britain.

18 Typical Belgic wheel-turned pottery from Colchester, Essex. The vessel on the left is the most distinctive Belgic product, a pedestal urn. That on the right is termed a 'tazza'. Both show the Belgic fondness for bead rims and smooth lines. Late first century BC–early first century AD

The apogee of the Belgic potters' craft was attained in the magnificent beakers produced at Colchester and probably elsewhere on the eve of the Roman invasion. In fine white and pinkish ware of almost eggshell thinness, they are tall, handle-less beer mugs ornamented on their swelling girths with patterns produced by running a toothed wheel (roulette) over the surface of the wet clay.

Trade and imports

The vigorous overseas trade which brought pottery from Gaul to grace the feasts of Belgic chiefs in south-east England between the time of Caesar and Claudius represents the culmination of centuries of buying and selling in Continental markets.

The list of foreign imports in Britain is impressive. They range from swords and horsegear to small personal objects of adornment and pots. Much of this trade probably flowed along well established routes. The most firmly established was that which operated from northern Europe across the North Sea. Almost as well established was the sea-borne trade from the Mediterranean and Spain to Cornwall and thence through the Irish Sea, a route which was still operating in the fifth and sixth centuries AD, bringing pottery from Africa and France. It was this route which brought Greek traders to Cornwall in search of tin – the trade is well documented by classical writers. Diodorus Siculus reported that

> In Britain the inhabitants of the promontory called Belerion are particularly friendly to strangers and have become civilized through contacts with traders from foreign parts. . . . They prepare the tin, working the ground in which it is produced, very carefully. . . . They beat the metal into masses shaped like astragali [knuckle bones] and carry it to a certain island lying off Britain called Ictis.

19 Iberian bronze figurine from Aust-on-Severn, Gloucestershire. Parallels in Spain are of the fourth–third centuries BC, and it may have been imported from there around this date. Made of bronze, with inlaid glass eyes, it is one of a series of objects suggesting contacts along the Atlantic coastal route in Iron Age Britain

This was probably the Isle of Wight, in and around which a concentration of Greek coins has been found; there are upwards of three hundred Greek coin finds in Britain, dating from the second and first centuries BC, a couple of which have been found in Iron Age contexts. A few other items support this picture of Mediterranean trade, including a bronze figurine of a lady from Spain, unearthed at Aust on the Severn, and some finds of Greek pottery from southern England. Were the three pots left in an artificial cave at Teignmouth, Devon, the votive offering of a sailor blown off course but thankful to be alive in the third century BC?

Most of the trade, however, relied on more direct routes. Over the Alps from Italy came objects such as a bronze corrugated bucket found at Weybridge, Surrey, and the bronze jugs of Etruscan origin from Northampton and the river Crouch in Essex, all of the fifth century BC. These no doubt represent an extension of the trade that brought

Mediterranean drinking vessels to the feasts of Hallstatt warriors in France and Germany. From Italy too came a series of safety-pin brooches, and from the heartland of the Continental Celts came bracelets and more exotic treasures such as the richly decorated hanging bowl from Cerrig-y-Drudion, the earliest example of La Tène art from the British Isles.

Much of this trade was conducted along fairly irregular lines, but there are hints that trading depots were established for the dissemination of goods by middlemen. One such post was at Hengistbury Head, Dorset, which conducted a vigorous trade with Armorica (Brittany) in the first century BC. In Hengistbury and its hinterland finds of Breton pottery have been densely distributed, and from the same region have come a variety of coins struck by Armorican tribes. This corroborates the reports by Strabo and Caesar of a healthy cross-Channel trade. One Armorican tribe in particular, the Veneti, are described as running a fleet of Channel boats (Caesar put a stop to both their political subversion and their trading activities when he defeated them in 56 BC).

The Britons of Hengistbury Head, however, had always been capable of carrying out trade on their own account: from the depot site and others within a 37-km radius fragments of amphorae (wine storage jars) have been unearthed that had come directly from Italy without passing through Venetic hands. One of these Italian ships went down off Belle-Isle, Morbihan, where it remains, its cargo still undrunk. Not surprisingly, this particular trade ceased after Caesar's mopping-up operations, though wine was once more taken through Celtic ports in the last years of the first century BC and the following decades. At the same time, such goods as Italian silver cups for quaffing wine were imported.

Settlements – hillforts

Hillforts are possibly the type of settlement most characteristically associated with the Iron Age, and yet the term covers a variety of sites from simple stock enclosures and massively-ramparted villages to developed ritual sites and the very advanced 'towns'.

Long before the Celts were a dominant force in Britain, all the elements for hillforts were already present. Hills had long been chosen as natural foci for tribal structure and for religious rites. High ground was often easy to fence or wall because of the natural layout, and no doubt there were psychological advantages in choosing a well-defined

natural feature such as a hill as the focus of one community. Hills too could be seen for long distances and almost certainly helped to keep the cohesion of scattered tribesmen in their hamlets or bothies. It is easy to understand how the Celts developed this type of settlement with its multi-purpose attraction.

Hillforts proper had been built in Britain at least five or six centuries before the first Celts arrived. They were substantial undertakings, with massive, squared ramparts faced front and back with upright timbers, tied by cross-beams. These box ramparts are best represented by the fine fort at Ivinghoe Beacon, Buckinghamshire, and they remained popular until at least the ninth century BC. They were probably difficult to construct and comparatively easy to

20 Univallate Iron Age hillfort at Uffington Castle, Berkshire, and the adjacent Uffington White Horse. On account of its similarity to some horses on Celtic British coins, and its proximity to the hillfort, it is usually assumed that this carving is of Iron Age date, and if so is the earliest of the chalk-cut figures in England

53

slight. A ready solution was to pile up a bank of earth behind the rampart in a slope which stabilized it and provided a good fighting platform. This was done at Hollingbury, Sussex, and seems to have been an innovation of around the sixth century BC. Hollingbury-type forts remained in use until the fourth century BC when they were ousted by even simpler ramparts in which the timbering was reduced to a front line anchored into the bank by tie beams, as at Poundbury, Dorset. The ultimate in rampart construction was the dump of *glacis* type, in which the bank sloped up gently from the bottom of the ditch in a single line of defence. This, in the absence of timbering, was impossible to fire and well-nigh impossible to slight. Such ramparts in various local forms were more or less universal from the third century BC in southern Britain.

It was during the very period that the Celts were first arriving on British shores that hillfort building was accelerated. The effect of similar Continental contacts on British building techniques is well illustrated from the distinctive traditions adopted in Iron Age north-east Scotland. The forts here had complex timber-laced ramparts and were faced front and rear by a carefully-built sheer stone wall. The rubble infilling was tied with cross-timbers. Their development can be associated with incomers from northern Germany, who are known from other distinctive products. The stone used was rich in silica which melts when subjected to intense heat. On accidental, or deliberate, firing by an enemy, the burning cross-beams inside the walls left draught channels through which cold air

21 The vitrified fort at Finavon, Angus. Such forts were constructed with timber lacing, which when fired either accidentally or on purpose created draught channels which melted or 'vitrified' the stone of the rampart itself. Finavon was made famous by Professor V. Gordon Childe's experiments to recreate its vitrifaction

could rush to the fire raging in the core of the rampart. The heat was raised to abnormally high temperatures, and the silica melted and fused into a solid mass. These 'vitrified' forts seemed difficult to explain until Professor V. G. Childe carried out a classic experiment in archaeology in 1937. He built a rampart of a basalt core faced with firebricks at Plean, Stirlingshire. Timber and brushwood were piled against it and at 11 a.m. on 11 March in a snowstorm, the flames were kindled. Aided by a 15 m.p.h. east wind, the fire blazed merrily for three hours before collapsing. The following morning observers noted that the mass had fused: the problem of how sufficient heat for vitrification in an Iron Age context had been possible was solved. Such vitrified forts were a feature of northern Scotland for several centuries after their first appearance.

Until around 500 BC both the north-west and the south-east of Britain had evolved along generally similar lines. The climatic deterioration which particularly afflicted the north-west and differing contacts with the Continent led increasingly from this time to a divergence between the two areas. In the fifth century contact between the south-east and Europe was at its maximum, and the southern British were becoming increasingly influenced by ideas from the La Tène world on the Continent – ideas which only slowly permeated northwards. Continental contacts were renewed at the end of the second century BC when further intensive development of hillforts occurred in the south. Some of this activity might have been a response to the arrival of the Belgae, some might have been due to their friendly

22 South Barrule hillfort, Isle of Man, from the air. A typical example of a multivallate hillfort, the hollows of many huts can be seen in the snow in the interior. Radiocarbon dating suggests occupation in the fifth century BC

influence. Either way, the southern Celts were obviously thrown into a ferment of defensive activity. The simple univallate hillforts were in some cases given further ramparts, others were elaborated into very complex structures. Some remained simple, and some were modified only in the last fifty years before the Roman conquest.

The weakest point in a hillfort's defences was its gate. Most forts had at least one of these, and Iron Age ingenuity was taxed to think out the solution to their defence. The earliest entrances have long corridor-like passages, as at Ivinghoe Beacon, which was entered by a passageway 3.4 m long of similar width. It was timber-lined and entered from a small courtyard formed by turning the ends of the ditch inward. Such entrances remained the norm until the fourth century BC, when it began to be felt that additional protection was needed. The solution was to construct flanking guard chambers of various types, perhaps inspired ultimately by concepts of classical Mediterranean gateways, or to set the gates further and further back. At the end of the second century BC gates were inturned to provide attenuated corridors, up to 45 m long, and some were provided with timber bridges. Ultimately, during the first century BC, complex outworks (called, after medieval castle architecture, barbicans) were added, to counteract a direct rush on the gate. These may have been evolved to handle the threat of capture by the Romans. Like the others of this type, the finest, Maiden Castle, Dorset, is in the west of England. In the first century, particularly in Kent, the Belgae developed a distinctive type of fort defence known after the

23 Maiden Castle, Dorset, from the air. This view shows the complex western entrance. The hollow slightly to the right of the centre of the picture is a well, the rectangular hollow slightly higher to its right is a dewpond. The bank in the extreme right bisecting the fort belongs to a Neolithic occupation of the site. Maiden Castle is the finest of the Iron Age hillforts in Britain, made famous by Sir Mortimer Wheeler's excavations there in the 1930s

classic site at Fécamp, France. They are distinguished by
having ditches with wide flat bottoms.

It is notable that these elaborate defensive structures, that must have required enormous feats of communal effort to build, were taken by the Romans within a few years of the conquest in 43, apparently with little difficulty. The Celts, unused to organized warfare, vainly hoped that massive ramparts and intricate gateways were enough to withstand civilization's forces. By the time that the Roman legions massed at the foot of the great Celtic hillforts of the south, the communities inside had developed from the simple stock rearers of the Bronze Age who had conceived of the idea of fencing kraals on high land. Hillforts of all types from the simple to the complex served a variety of needs that reflected the more advanced society. They were defensive, they were stock enclosures, they were religious centres and assembly points for the population. But they were also the scene of industry and manufacture of goods, and the obvious sites for markets. Here judgment was made and the chief held sway. In short they were the political, economic, social and religious foci for the many tribes and were adapted and modified according to needs and supplies. It is remarkable that studies of the distribution of hillforts on the South Downs and in the Chilterns show that each major fort dominated a territorial block of about 64 sq. km. Lesser forts were no doubt ruled by sub-chiefs.

It is an indication of the organization of Celtic society on the eve of the Roman conquest that some forts display evidence of deliberate planning policies, presumably by some centralized authority for community affairs. At Danebury, Hants, at Croft Ambrey, Credenhill Camp and Midsummer Hill in the Welsh Marches, and at Crickley Hill in Gloucestershire, there is abundant evidence for rectangular buildings being set in lines along 'streets'. On all these sites, houses were rebuilt many times on the same spot, demonstrating continuity both of controlled 'town planning' and of occupation. At Danebury five rows of buildings were uncovered, all parallel to the rampart, with an area left clear behind for storage and rubbish pits. Within the forts there is evidence for zoning – particular regions were devoted to specialist activities such as metalworking, grain storage or domestic habitation.

The forts of southern Britain seem to have enjoyed more or less continuous occupation. It is less clear whether this was also the case in the north, where there might have been transhumance from lowland settlements to upland forts on a seasonal basis. Seasonal or not, the density of occupation in forts of highland Britain was not less than in the south. Calculations on surviving stone built huts at Tre'er Ceiri and Garn Boduan in Gwynedd, indicate a population of 500 or more, while at Traprain Law, East Lothian, the number is more likely to have approached 3,000.

On the eve of the Roman conquest the Belgic chiefs of the south had achieved a standard of living akin to true urbanization. Caesar distinguished two types of larger nucleated settlement in Gaul, *oppida* (towns) and *urbes* (cities). In Britain he saw only *oppida*, but it seems very probable that settlements he would have called *urbes* had evolved within the quarter century after his visits. To qualify as an *oppidum* in Caesar's view, all a settlement required was a rampart and ditch: to qualify for urban status it had to be a tribal centre. The settlements in the Belgic areas of Britain that are known as *oppida* (of which some might eventually have attained the status of *urbes*) differ from the hillforts in that they are frequently sited on low-lying ground, and are enclosed with an earthwork which may not be continuous, and may utilize natural defences in its circuit. Like the hillforts, they were industrial, political and economic centres, the foci of far-flung trade.

On some sites evidence for mints has come to light. Coin moulds and other mint debris were found in the important tribal centres of St Albans, Colchester, Bagendon, Silchester and elsewhere; these sites have also produced a variety of Roman and Gallo-Belgic imports, as well as evidence for industrial activity. This is very well illustrated from the Sheepen site near Colchester, the capital of king Cunobelin of the Catuvellauni. Here the entire settlement was protected by a series of earthworks set out in straight lines to define a territory some 22 sq. km in extent. How many habitations lay within this area is unknown – it is inconceivable that the whole area was occupied – but even the half mile or so that was excavated represents an extensive occupation. Some round, some rectangular huts with their ditches, gullies and pits were scattered in the area. One small area was so rich in imported pottery that the excavator suggested that it must have been the residence of king Cunobelin himself. Inscribed potsherds suggest that at least one of the residents was literate and knew the Latin alphabet. Some of the inscriptions may, however, have been graffiti scrawled by visitors to Cunobelin's court. From this period onwards, the Celts start to make themselve remembered in the annals of history as well as the archaeological records.

Not all the settlements were on the scale of hillforts and *oppida*. Smaller but still nucleated settlement is represented by the villages of stone huts that are found on the extremities of Celtic Britain, in Cornwall and the Northern Isles. The most famous, justly so, are Carn Euny and Chysauster in Cornwall and Jarlshof in Shetland. In both these areas the settlements are very obvious responses to the environment.

The atmosphere at Chysauster is as ghostly as a Highland Clearance village of Scotland. It lies on a bleak moorland reached by narrow Cornish roads, the empty, stone-walled houses blending in with the landscape, their gardens

24 Chysauster, a native settlement near Penzance, Cornwall, from the air. The village consists of four pairs of houses, with a ninth on its own. Each house had an open courtyard, from which rooms opened out. The adjacent terraces were probably gardens. Occupied from the first century BC until *c.*AD 300

reverted to heath. The house type is distinctive of the south-west peninsula, with a central courtyard from which the rooms open out. There are four pairs of houses and a ninth standing on its own. All have adjacent terraces which were probably the gardens. The open courtyard was approached by an entrance passage and the rooms, which were roofed from a central pole set in a socket-stone, were in effect little individual huts. Breton influence has been suggested to account for their plans, and they were occupied from the first century BC, until their abandonment well in the Roman period in about AD 300. Nearby is the field system that supported the community.

Not far away is Carn Euny where excavation showed that stone huts of the first century BC replaced timber dwellings. One of the Carn Euny houses features a *fogou* or under-ground cellar (there is a more ruined example too at Chysauster). A gallery, 1.83 m high and 1.53 m wide, leads to it from one house, and is still roofed with its massive

59

capstones. The *fogou* itself is round and once had a corbelled dome. It was probably used as a store – perhaps for keeping meat or dairy produce cool, for pastoralism was more important than agriculture in Iron Age Cornwall. Only some of these early Cornishmen lived in villages. Others lived in single farmsteads set in a circular rampart. They are known as *rounds* and occur all over the county. Since there are over a thousand the spacing seems to have been of one to every square mile.

25 Interior of *fogou*, Carn Euny, Cornwall. *Fogous* were a Cornish version of a widespread type of Iron Age structure, the 'earthhouse' or 'souterrain'. Usually connected to an above-ground hut, some may have served as store-rooms (perhaps for dairy produce) or as places of retreat. This example is in a village similar to that at Chysauster, where a ruined *fogou* was also found. Carn Euny, as recent re-excavation has shown, was occupied from the fifth century BC onwards, and it has been suggested that this *fogou* may have had a ritual function, perhaps for the worship of an 'underground' deity

In lowland Britain the houses themselves were mainly built in timber and display distinctive plans. One of the most common is the 'round hut', a term used by archaeologists to describe a considerable diversity of homes ranging from large and complex dwellings down to small huts only 3.7–4.6 m across. There is also growing evidence for the existence of rectangular timber buildings, of which the largest are those excavated in the hillfort at Crickley, Glos, which were up to 18 m long.

Of the round houses, the most complex are similar to the one excavated at the famous Iron Age site of Little Woodbury, Wilts. Houses in this tradition were first built in Bronze Age Britain, and, although the most elaborate are in Wessex, related structures have been found elsewhere, as for instance at West Brandon, Co. Durham. The house at Little Woodbury was nearly 4.6 m in diameter with a double concentric line of postholes, the outer representing the supports for the outside wall, the inner for the roof. The house was entered through a porch and passage, which may have been designed to provide a double door as a fire protection – if one door was closed before the other was opened there was far less risk of a sudden draught blowing sparks from the central hearth to set the thatched roof on fire. Little Woodbury was unusual in that it had a setting of four posts, which may have been the remains of a central tower, the loft of which might have been a store. This would have simplified the problems of roofing the large area. It has also been suggested, however, that the roof was open to the sky. Whatever the finished structure, the houses need not have been scruffy. The walls would have been of wattle and daub which could have been painted as were the German houses described by Tacitus. The roofs might have been

26 A reconstruction of an Iron Age house as part of the Butser Ancient Farm Project, Hampshire. This house is based on one excavated at Pimperne, Dorset. The Butser Project is an extensive research programme to investigate Iron Age methods of farming, and involves animal husbandry and crop growing as well as experiments in the usage of storage pits. The site chosen for the project was one which had been used in the Iron Age

thatched ornamentally and the woodwork could have been carved.

The house at Little Woodbury stood within a complex of enclosures. The immediate vicinity of the house with its pits, working areas and granaries, was demarcated by a ditch about 1.8 m deep and 2.7 m across. A palisade ran round the inside of the ditch except at the entrance. The site covered about 8.6 ha and outside lay 'antenna' ditches which were probably a droveway for channelling stock into the compound. Other ditches spanned the area between this and another enclosure known as Greater Woodbury which was about 24.7 ha in extent. Rectilinear stock compounds lay to the north-east of Little Woodbury.

The farm complex was as exceptional as the house itself but various types of enclosures containing houses were common in the south generally and associated with arable fields, pasture and sometimes a network of connecting trackways.

In the north of Britain the climate led to different types of settlements. There is a fortuitous similarity between the courtyard houses of Cornwall and the stone houses of the

Northern Isles which is due to the lack of timber common to the two areas. The Iron Age remains of Atlantic Scotland are among the most impressive in Britain and the round stone towers known as brochs which developed in the first century BC have reasonable claim to be among the most outstanding structures of their period in Northern Europe. The development of building techniques is best demonstrated from the two Shetland sites of Jarlshof and Clickhimin which together provide a history of continuous

27 Late Bronze Age and early Iron Age 'villages', Jarlshof, Shetland. Superficially similar to Chysauster, the characteristic house was of 'courtyard' type, with small rooms leading off a central court. In the hut in the foreground can be seen a saddle quern for grinding grain (another can be seen outside the hut wall at the bottom left) and hearths. The trapdoor on the right covers the entrance to a late Bronze Age souterrain, the earliest in Britain. The hut in the foreground is hut IV of the settlement. Seventh–sixth century BC

habitation from the Neolithic to the Middle Ages.

Jarlshof is one of the longest-occupied sites in Britain. It lies at the most southerly tip of the Shetland mainland, a short walk from the airport of Sumburgh. It is a veritable British Pompeii: the successive settlements were engulfed by sand which preserved the structures and their contents to a remarkable degree. After Neolithic occupation, a village of stone 'courtyard houses' was built only to be abandoned by the late Bronze Age when a smith set up his workshop in one of the ruined buildings.

On top of the ruins another village was gradually built in the fifth century BC. One of the villagers was a blacksmith, for slag was among the finds. The houses were circular and had stone piers set radially to support the roof. This settlement was in turn abandoned, and Jarlshof was not reoccupied until the stone towers known as brochs had evolved.

The gap in habitation at Jarlshof can be filled from the discoveries at Clickhimin which now lies on an islet in a loch in a suburb of Shetland's capital, Lerwick. The first building on the site was a late Bronze Age courtyard house similar to those at Jarlshof. This was still in use when the inhabitants of the site centuries later had started to use pottery of a characteristic Shetland Iron Age type. In the fifth century BC or slightly later newcomers enclosed the still inhabited courtyard house in a stone fort with a massive carefully constructed wall. Around the inside of this were timber ranges in which no doubt cattle were stalled and people lived. Early in the first century BC the inhabitants decided to improve their fort by building a new inner ringwork,

28 The 'blockhouse' at Clickhimin, Shetland. Constructed as the entrance to an unfinished stone-walled fort, it shows many features– such as hollow walling and intra-mural staircase and chambers–of the later brochs, which evolved out of such structures. Originally the blockhouse stood three storeys high, and had internal timber ranges. Second century BC

entered through a 'blockhouse' with flanking guard-chambers and hollow walling. The blockhouse passage was closed with a wooden door fastened with a bar, and a stairway gave access to the top and no doubt also to the wall-walk of the ringwork.

This type of fortification is of some significance because it was an elaboration of Hebridean stone-walled forts. Subsequently the type developed into what are known as brochs, the very distinctive Iron Age Scottish towers built in the first centuries BC and AD. These were introduced into the Northern Isles from the Hebrides and eventually a broch replaced the inner ringwork at Clickhimin during the first century AD.

Brochs are found mainly in the Western and Northern Isles of Scotland and on the northern mainland. They are the Iron Age equivalent of fortified residences or 'castles'. By far the finest is the Broch of Mousa, which has survived due to its inaccessible siting on a now uninhabited island off the east coast of Shetland. It rises 13.1 m above the rocks on the island's shore. Like all brochs it is entered by a single door flanked by guard-chambers. Timber ranges were built

29 The Broch of Mousa, Shetland. Still standing over 12 m high, this stone tower is typical of the brochs of northern Scotland, built in the first century BC–first century AD, which developed out of earlier types of stone-walled forts

30 Intra-mural staircase, the broch of Midhowe, Orkney. This shows the building skill of the broch people

round the inside walls supported on a casement ledge above ground level. Since there was a well to collect rainwater the centre of the court was probably open to the sky. The timber galleries were reached by stairs inside the wall which rise unevenly to the top between the two 'skins' of the wall, which are tied together by cross-stones. This distinctive

31 Reconstruction of Clickhimin in the broch period, by Alan Sorrell. The blockhouse and stone-walled fort of the earlier Iron Age can be seen in the centre. A broch was built within the enclosure fairly late in its history. It was built near the edge of a loch

32 Interior of the broch of Gurness, Aikerness, Orkney. The single entrance to the broch tower can be seen at the back of the picture. In the foreground is the central well. The slab partitions were erected after the broch was abandoned, when the interior was occupied by wheelhouse-period squatters

method of building produced galleries inside the walls, dark corridors which can still be crawled along with the aid of a torch and stout nerves. Because of the height of the walls the courtyard of the Mousa broch is dank and gloomy even on a sunny day and must have been even more so when the space was reduced by the presence of the timber ranges.

65

Two Viking lovers are known to have hidden in this tower centuries later.

The Brochs of Mousa and Clickhimin remained in occupation until perhaps as late as the second century AD. The age of the brochs was a violent period in Scottish history. Among the finds from the Orcadian Broch of Gurness, Aikerness, were the bones of two hands that had been deliberately severed at the wrist. Three rings remained on the finger of one hand, two on the finger of the other. Roman objects from many brochs might suggest raiding further south, for these remote areas remained Celtic throughout the Iron Age into the Dark Ages without hearing the tramp of Roman soldiers.

Not much is known about the weapons of the broch warriors, for iron does not survive well in the northern climate, but they seem to have used fire-spears – socketed bone tips attached to wooden shafts with bundles of inflammable material. Fire-spears have also been found in England, one coming from the warrior burial at Grimsthorpe, Yorks. They also used slingstones, painted with various signs and symbols that may have had some purpose as a talisman. The Greeks and Romans used a similar device on some of their lead slingshot, which had inscriptions such as 'Strike Hard' on them.

From the second century AD onwards a more peaceful state of affairs prevailed. The brochs fell into ruin, and round stone huts were built by the later generations, sometimes with stones robbed from the brochs. At Jarlshof the post-broch people must have lived in constant danger from the falling masonry. In Shetland a distinctive type of stone hut, known as a wheelhouse, evolved. It was somewhat reminiscent of its earlier Iron Age precursors, but probably not directly related. Piers set radially supported the roof, and the 'hub' of the wheel was taken up with a central fireplace. Such wheelhouses were inhabited continuously until the coming of the Vikings and reinforce the picture of remarkable continuity of occupation in Atlantic Scotland during the Celtic period, when the rest of Britain was disturbed by the arrival of the Romans.

Celtic art

In the Basse-Yutz flagons, now in the British Museum, can be seen all the elements that went into creating Celtic art. The flagons borrow elements from the Classical world, and also improve on them. The model for the artist was the type of bulbous wine jug that was being imported in the fifth century BC from Etruscan Italy, to grace Celtic feasts. But

the Celtic artist has not been content in slavishly following the original form. From the carefully moulded foot the jugs blossom upwards, their sides concave, to reach the smooth angle of the shoulder. Drawn in, the necks carry the eye upwards and open out in the beaked spout. The handles are fabulous beasts, which grip the ornamental lids with their forepaws, and are chained to them from their mouths. Where the 'handle' meets the shoulder of the vessel there stares out a moustachioed Celtic face, its eyebrows bushy and curling in arabesques which match the curls of its beard. The eyes were once set with coral, and coral once red, now white, is set in a pattern which seems a foretaste of the interlace so beloved of Celtic artists centuries later. On the spout a little duck swims towards the stream of wine and a pair of mythical creatures recline on either side of the neck.

The Basse-Yutz flagons date from the late fifth or early fourth century BC, when the earliest La Tène style was emerging. They are a source-book for Celtic art in themselves, for on them can be detected all the major influences that were to crystallize into the mature La Tène style.

33 The Basse-Yutz flagons. Superb examples of Continental Celtic art, these flagons are modelled on contemporary or slightly earlier Etruscan wide jugs. They date from the late fifth or early fourth century BC, when the earliest style of La Tène art was emerging, and were found in Moselle, Lorraine

Even details stem from Mediterranean civilization; the facing mask on the handle is nothing less than a Celticized Silenos of Classical wine jugs, and the palmette motifs too have a Classical origin. The creature which forms the handle has a more involved pedigree. It is probably a dog, and its pointed ears, its curving shoulder spiral used to denote muscle, and its hatched fur all point directly to the world of the Scythian nomads of the Steppe. The hatching is probably a modification of a woodworking technique and the shoulder spiral haunted European art till the age of the Vikings. But the dog, though inspired directly from Scythian work, can also be found in ancient Persian art, which may also provide the original inspiration for the beasts on the neck. The duck, on the other hand, is more homely. Its predecessors were cult objects in Hallstatt Europe. Here it is simply ornamental, a piece of whimsical good humour.

The Basse-Yutz flagons were found by workmen in 1927. The story goes that they were offered to the Louvre, who refused to buy them on the grounds that they were too fine to be genuine, and who had been taken in by forgeries of similar articles in the too recent past. The British Museum bought them and they were proved to be authentic. Thus it happens that two of the finest treasures to come out of Celtic Gaul are now in a glass case in London.

Classical Mediterranean, Scythian, Persian and native Hallstatt, then, were some of the influences in the emergence of Celtic art. Another was *situla art,* a style which evolved at the head of the Adriatic and was partly Classical and partly barbarian with strong Oriental influence. As its name suggests, it was used in the decoration of bronze buckets or *situlae,* which were traded over the Alps where they were seen by Celtic artists.

Out of these diverse sources Celtic art emerged, new, vigorous and exciting, in the fourth century BC, after a phase of experimentation termed the *Early style.* Its first distinctive phase is the *Waldalgesheim,* named after a rich double grave in Germany, in which the style is well represented on a series of fine torcs and bracelets. The Waldalgesheim grave dates from the fourth century BC, and here the symmetry of the patterns borrowed from Greek plant ornament has been disturbed. Strong relief ornament and human masks are two features of the earlier Waldalgesheim style. Human masks featured in the mature Waldalgesheim phase, but were replaced by a fine sense of patterning. It was this style that was the first to be transmitted to Britain, on objects such as the hanging bowl from Cerrig-y-Drudion. It developed into the *Insular* Celtic styles.

Meanwhile, in Continental Europe, the Waldalgesheim was being supplanted by what was once termed the *Plastic style* because of the artists' delight in high relief moulding. More recently it has been renamed the *Disney style* (by Prof. J. V. S. Megaw) on account of its rich use of joke motifs and *double entendre* in its visual imagery. It uses the same kind of visual punning that is employed in the twentieth century, the images being broken up into constituent elements which can be seen as patterns or faces, usually animal rather than human.

Overlapping with the Plastic style was the *Sword style*, which takes its name from its use in two-dimensional engraved work on sword scabbards and other objects, set in asymmetrical patterns. Both Plastic and Sword styles belong to the third century BC, by which time coinage was making its appearance in Europe and thenceforth remained a medium for Celtic art until the coming of Caesar. The Gallic wars put an end to the rich patronage of Celtic artists by their chiefs, and with the Romanization of Gaul, Celtic art had effectively died out.

The insular styles

In Britain, Celtic art was only just coming into existence in the third century BC. It was not until after the coming of the Belgae that distinctive native styles evolved, for it was the patronage of these overlords that provided the Celtic British artists with the scope to innovate and experiment.

The first introduction of Celtic art to the Britons came with some Continental imports and subsequent native imitations. The earliest manifestations of native style have a great deal in common with Continental Sword style work, and appropriately many examples are to be found on sword scabbards. The Wisbech scabbard plate, with its fleshy scroll pattern of split palmettes, may be an import but could as easily be the product of a western British workshop. It shows echoes of the ornament on the Cerrig-y-Drudion bowl. So too does the bracelet found in a 'chariot' burial at Newnham Croft, Cambridgeshire, one of the very few Continental-style chariot burials recorded outside the Arras group (p. 10). The grave was found in 1903, and contained the body of a middle-aged man accompanied by an odd array of possessions. The most tasteless was a brooch decorated with coral studs in a native version of the Plastic style, which could be dated to the third or second century BC. Another of the grave goods was an armlet with elongated low relief Waldalgesheim ornament, a pony cap with dingle-dangles to tinkle as the animal cantered, some rings possibly from a pony harness, and a couple of penannular brooches. The collection points to a date in the third or second century BC for the burial, the time when Continental ideas were being increasingly adopted and adapted by British workshops.

In the second century insular schools were established: in the south the Witham shield and sword, and later the Battersea shield (p. 24) show distinctive features, and eastern smiths produced the Torrs pony cap and horn mounts.

The Torrs horn mounts are worth closer scrutiny. They were designed as finials for drinking horns which were perhaps made from the crowning glory of an aurochs, the now extinct wild ox which roamed Iron Age forests. The horn mounts terminate in naturalistic duck heads, their distinctive beaks showing them to be shovellers, the winter visitors and summer residents to be seen in many parts of modern Britain. The ornament is very neatly incised and very elaborate; each pattern begins with a circular *yin-yang* element and swells outwards into a central design before

34 The Torrs horns, Kelton, Kirkcudbright. Now attached to the Torrs pony cap (Plate 8), they may have been the tips of drinking horns (compare the birds' heads with those on the drinking horn held by the Pict on Plate 79). The design engraved on them is distinctively early (mid-second century BC) and extremely graceful. The bird is probably a shoveller duck

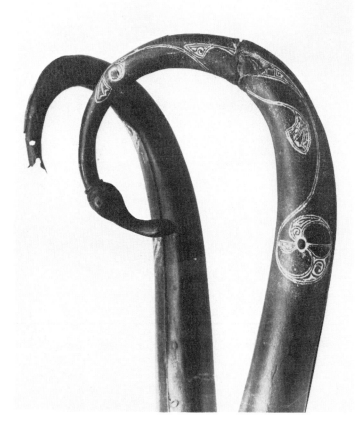

tailing off into a delicate fan-shaped tip. A tiny full-face human mask has been incorporated into the central element of the larger horn. There is almost a Dark Age aura about the horns. A similar drinking vessel, complete with duck's head terminal, is brandished by a drunken Pict on a sculpture nearly a thousand years later, a reminder of Celtic conservatism.

Of similar second century BC date, the shield bosses from Wandsworth, London, dredged up from the river Thames, acclaim the achievements of the southern workshops. The finer of the two is circular, with a pattern of foliate ornament and ducks' heads – 'obsessive birds hatched from a Hallstatt egg in the central La Tène province' (N. K. Sandars, *Prehistoric Art*, Harmondsworth, 1968) – effected in relief around the central dome, which is itself richly ornamented with engraved patterns recalling the Torrs horns.

Chronologically overlapping with such pieces are the series of ornamental swords and scabbards (p. 27). Of the later scabbards one is particularly worth singling out: the

35 Shield boss from Wandsworth, London, combining repoussé ornament with engraving of Torrs type. The central roundel is delicately engraved, and the style is similar to that seen at Torrs. Late second or early first century BC. Diameter 33 cm

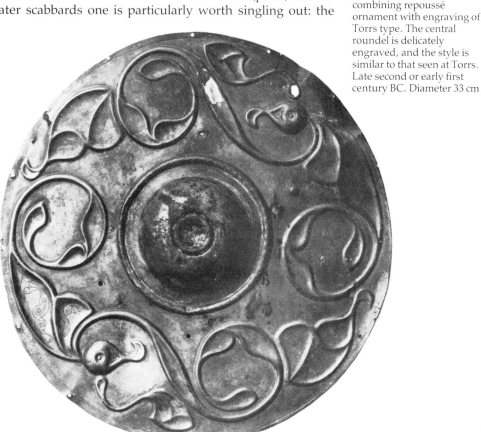

Bugthorpe scabbard was found in a burial in the East Riding of Yorkshire and dates from around 100 BC. Although this nineteenth-century find has its Yorkshire counterparts, such as the example found at Grimthorpe in 1868, all were probably made in the south and taken north by refugees fleeing from the Belgic immigrants. The back plate of the Bugthorpe scabbard is of iron, its front of bronze, richly ornamented with a wealth of engraved detail. The chape, with its fleshy bifid tip, recalls the pouting mouth of a fish,

36 Bronze and iron scabbard, Bugthorpe, Yorkshire. Perhaps made in the late first century BC by refugee craftsmen from the south-east, the style of its ornament is similar to that on the Datchet spearhead (Plate 6). Length: 61.5 cm

and when turned sideways, its curvilinear ornament takes on the appearance of an eye. The art is totally abstract, the voids being infilled with carefully executed basketry.

Basketry infilling is a feature of what had, arguably, reached the pinnacle of British Celtic artistic achievements – the mirrors produced in the late first century BC and early first century AD for the Belgic aristocracy. The inspiration behind them is Roman and is manifested in the symmetrical, ordered arrangement of the pattern on the mirror backs. The series is difficult to localize, for though most have been found in the south-east, there is evidence that they were made in the territory of the Cotswold tribe of the Dobunni. So distinctive is this decoration that it is known as the *Mirror style*, though it also appears on other objects, such as the spearhead from Datchet (p. 28).

An early example of the style is the Mayer Mirror, which takes its name from a famous nineteenth-century Liverpool collector who owned it for a while. On this piece the ornament is arranged in three circles, and the handle is a loop with a skeuomorphic binding in the centre, like cane-work.

Far more advanced are the mirrors from Birdlip, Glos, and Desborough, Northants. They have elaborate handles cast in one and fastened on to the mirror plate. On these the pattern has opened out, flower-like, into an overall scheme of breath-taking ingenuity. The Birdlip Mirror was found during road building, in a lady's grave at Birdlip Hill. In 1953

37 Grave group from Birdlip, Gloucestershire. The mirror is typical of those produced in the south-east, and the other objects comprise two beaten bronze bowls, a safety-pin brooch with bird's head (named after this example the 'Birdlip' type), a tubular bronze bracelet, a necklace of amber, jet and marble beads and a bronze handle with its terminal in the shape of a horned animal. The grave, which belonged to a woman, was found in a limestone cist in 1879 during quarrying. It dates from the early first century AD. Height of mirror: *c*.38.7 cm

38 The Desborough (Northants) mirror. One of the finest of the mirrors produced in south-east England for the Belgic nobles' ladies, its back is decorated with basketry pattern arranged symmetrically, due to Roman influence. Early first century AD or late first century BC. Height: *c*.35 cm

British Museum conservators engaged on restoring the piece revealed that under the handle a basketry pattern had been 'tried out' by the artist to see the general effect of his tooling before he began the final design.

Many types of object received the attention of Belgic

73

artists. Openwork modelling similar to that on the mirror handles can be seen on a series of tankard handles. The Trawsfynydd handle is still attached to the original tankard. The vessel itself is an object of noteworthy stylishness. Professor J. V. S. Megaw has compared its handle to a balustrade by Charles Rennie Mackintosh, summing it up as a 'fine example of pre-Christian "art nouveau" ', which indeed it is. The profile is gently curved, and it is made of wood staves with a turned wooden base, the sides being

39 Tankard of bronze-bound yew staves from Trawsfynydd, Gwynedd (formerly Merioneth). Typical of a series of Belgic tankards of which usually only the ornamental handles survived, this magnificent vessel may have foamed with beer at many a Celtic feast. The design of the handle shows the way in which Belgic design was extended to relatively functional objects. Mid-first century AD. Height: 14.3 cm. Diameter: 18.3 cm

cased in sheet-bronze. Even the underside of the Trawsfynydd tankard is pleasing, with a double circle of wavy bronze wire hammered into the wood to provide a pattern which sets off the double circle of turned ornament and the central bronze roundel. Two other complete tankards survive, but they display far less style. That from Shapwick Heath, Somerset, looks like a reject from a third-rate Victorian public house, while the other, from the river Thames at Kew, resembles a diminutive oil drum with a handle added as an afterthought.

A lavish Celtic feast would not have been complete without firedogs of wrought iron, designed to carry a spit above a fire. Characteristically they are decorated with ox heads. The most ornate that has been found came from Capel Garmon, North Wales, and is almost Victorian in its florid use of ornament, the ox with its head down, its nostrils flared and its mouth open in a bellow as though about to charge – the horns are long and vicious.

Wrought iron generally was a Belgic speciality. Few more accomplished works of the smith have come down to us than the massive, 2.3 m long cauldron chain from Great Chesterford, Essex, which surpasses the later but comparable Anglo-Saxon chain from the Sutton Hoo ship burial. It turned freely on a swivel to which iron cords were attached, elaborated with hooks. From these a chain of double links cascaded, caught at the centre in an iron reef knot, to which the cauldron hooks were attached with

40 Firedog for roasting spits over a hearth, Capel Garmon, Denbigh. Height: about 75 cm. The terminals, in keeping with Belgic tradition, are decorated with bull's heads. This is a good example of Belgic skill with wrought ironwork

further chains. Although found in a Roman rubbish pit of the fourth century AD, it is of Celtic workmanship and undoubtedly hung from the rafters of some Celtic chief's home.

Unlike their predecessors, Belgic artists adored animal heads as ornamental devices. Ox or bull heads appear as handle attachments on firedogs and buckets, and bronze bowls had animal spouts or handles. A ram's head adorns a bronze bowl from Youlton, Cornwall, and a fish-head forms the spout of a bowl from Felmersham-on-Ouse, Bedfordshire. Rams appear on a tub from Harpenden, Essex. A horse head on a chariot mount from Stanwick, Yorkshire, so gained the approval of the eminent art historian Sir Cyril Fox that he pronounced that 'never was bland, smug, full-fed stable horsiness better delineated'.

Ducks are ubiquitous. One of the finest is a small bronze found with other models of a stag and a song-bird from the fort rampart at Milber, Devon. The duck prompted Fox to

41 Series of bronze mounts from a hoard found at Stanwick, Yorkshire. The hoard, datable to the first century AD, comprised native horse and chariot fittings and was found near the Brigantian stronghold excavated after the Second World War. The repoussé harness mounts here shown include a fine representation of a horse (*right*). Height of horse: *c*.10.9 cm

observe that 'it is not just a "duck", it is a duck swimming, alert and expecting interference, because it has a griddle cake in its bill . . . it is "essential duckery" expressed in the simplest terms' (*Pattern and Purpose: Early Celtic Art in Britain,* Cardiff, 1958, p. 79).

The Hounslow Boar is another bronze in true Celtic spirit, which captures with great economy of detail the character of a wild pig.

The rich diversity of Celtic art under the Belgae is best appreciated by considering two metalwork hoards from north Wales. The more recent discovery came to light in June 1963 on the slopes of Nant Cader, Merioneth, over-looking Tal-y-Llyn lake. It was found by two picnickers, who happened to stop for tea and noticed some pieces of sheet bronze half buried under a large boulder. On unearthing these, they found them to be part of a tightly packed bundle that had been hammered down for remelting. The hoard consisted of mounts for two shields, a pair of trapezoidal plaques ornamented with double human figures, and four composite bronze discs each of openwork fastened to a back plate, of which the original function is unknown. The additional presence of a Roman lock plate suggests concealment by a tinker in the first century AD. The main

42 Bronze boar, Hounslow, Middlesex. Found with other figurines including boars, it is probably a votive figure for a shrine, as boars were revered by the Celts. Late first century BC or early first century AD. Length: approx 7.6 cm

43 Bronze repoussé plaque, from a hoard found at Tal-y-Llyn, Gwynedd (Merioneth) in 1963. Max. width: 10.4 cm. This probably once adorned a shield, and may depict severed heads – the Celts were head-hunters. Late first century BC–early first century AD

artistic element displayed in the hoard is the triskele, the three-legged pattern that continued in popularity through the Roman period and became the main element in the re-emergent art of Dark Age Britain.

The larger hoard was found during the construction of a runway in 1942, when peat was required for bottoming and a nearby bog was dredged at Llyn Cerrig Bach, Anglesey. The first find to be pulled up by the harrow was the iron chain used for dragging lorries out of the mud (p. 20). It was followed by bones and about 150 Iron Age objects. These were likely to be only a small proportion of those originally thrown into the bog as offerings to now unknown gods.

The range of the finds is staggering; there are swords, pieces of a dagger, spears, a shield boss, the tyres, nave-hoops, pole-tip, cap and lynch pins of chariots, various horse trappings, gang-chains, currency bars, tongs, a sickle, cauldrons, a trumpet, bronze ribbons from ash staves and a series of finely decorated bronze mounts of unknown function. The collection had been accumulated slowly from the second century BC until the middle of the first century AD and objects had originated in south-east and south-west England and from Ireland.

If one object were to be chosen from the group as representative of Celtic art, it should doubtless be the crescentic plaque of bronze which probably ornamented the point at which the pole meets the body of a chariot. Dating from early in the first century BC, it is decorated with relief patterns in which the central element is the triskele. The

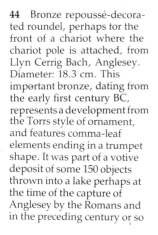

44 Bronze repoussé-decorated roundel, perhaps for the front of a chariot where the chariot pole is attached, from Llyn Cerrig Bach, Anglesey. Diameter: 18.3 cm. This important bronze, dating from the early first century BC, represents a development from the Torrs style of ornament, and features comma-leaf elements ending in a trumpet shape. It was part of a votive deposit of some 150 objects thrown into a lake perhaps at the time of the capture of Anglesey by the Romans and in the preceding century or so

composition was carefully laid out with the aid of compasses though the asymmetrical final result obscures the mathematical origins (this is a feature of the great Dark Age Celtic manuscripts such as the Book of Kells). The Llyn Cerrig plaque uses the *yin-yang* structure and explores voids as elements of the decorative whole. It is at once simple and complex, traditional and individualistic, ornamental and symbolic.

Celtic religion

When archaeologists were excavating the Iron Age and Romano-British temple at Harlow, Essex, they found a coin of Cunobelin in the gravel of the Iron Age foundation. The design on the reverse was indisputable; it showed an aproned but otherwise naked man holding a severed human head in one hand and a sceptre in the other. Was this an Iron Age representation of a druid going about his grisly business? If so, coins like this one are the only instances of such depictions from the period.

For other aspects of Celtic religion, however, there is plenty of evidence, some of it grotesque, some mundane, a great deal of it enigmatic. What is to be made of the writings of Classical authors about Celtic religion and its priests the druids? What deductions can be drawn from the human

(a)

(b)

45 Celtic British coins depicting priests. The bronze coin of Cunobelin (a) has as its reverse type a naked priest wearing what appears to be an apron, perhaps of leather, and carrying a severed head. Behind can be seen an 'altar'. Is this evidence for human sacrifice? Struck at Colchester, the reverse carries the CAM (ulodunum) mint name. The obverse is a sphinx, inspired by a classical prototype. The obverse is a sphinx, inspired by a classical prototype. (b) A bronze coin struck by Tasciovanus at St Albans (the VER(ulamium) mint name can be seen in the exergue on the reverse). The obverse is a classical-style bust, the reverse depicts a figure, probably a priest, making an offering at a bowl on a stem. Behind the throne are faint traces of a post, which on some specimens appears to be a stylized tree, perhaps indicative of a sacrifice being made in a grove. From casts of coins in the British Museum

skulls, the wooden effigies, the ritual pits and bizarre carvings provided by archaeology? And what kernel of truth, if any, lies behind the fantasies of eighteenth-century romantics?

The most useful starting point for any quest for Celtic gods is the writings of Caesar on the subject of the druids. As he wrote in *The Conquest of Gaul* (trans. S. A. Handford, Harmondsworth, 1951):

> The druids officiate at the worship of the gods, regulate public and private sacrifices, and give rulings on all religious questions. Large numbers of young men flock to them for instruction, and they are held in great honour by the people. They act as judges in practically all disputes, whether between tribes or individuals; when any crime is committed, or a murder takes place, or a dispute arises about an inheritance or a boundary, it is they who adjudicate the matter and appoint the compensation to be paid and received by the parties concerned. . . . All the druids are under one head, whom they hold in the highest respect . . . the Druidic doctrine is believed to have been found existing in Britain and thence imported into Gaul; even today those who want to make a profound study of it generally go to Britain for the purpose. The Druids are exempt from military service and do not pay taxes like other citizens. These important privileges are naturally attractive: many present themselves of their own accord to become students of druidism, and others are sent by their parents and relatives. It is said that these pupils have to memorize a great number of verses – so many, that some of them spend twenty years at their studies. . . . A lesson they take particular pains to inculcate is that the soul does not perish, but after death passes from one body to another; they think that this is the best incentive to bravery, because it teaches men to disregard the terrors of death. They also hold long discussion about the heavenly bodies and their movements, the size of the universe and of the earth, the physical constitution of the world, and the power and properties of the gods; and they instruct the young men in all these subjects.

This description has been quoted at some length because it is the origin for most of the later traditions about the druids. Although it contains much which is no doubt quite true, it is also misleading, for Caesar was trying to interpret something which he but dimly understood and which had to be rationalized into terms intelligible to his urbane readers. He is no doubt right when he says the druids were powerful men whose authority covered religious matters and extended to legal issues. He is no doubt correct too in saying that there was an arch-druid, that Britain was pre-eminent in druidic matters, and that there were schools for the instruction of the young in druidic lore, passed on by word of mouth. It is highly unlikely, however, that the druids believed in the transmigration of souls. This probably stems from a misinterpretation of the Celtic love of transformations – Celtic literature abounds with miraculous transmutations of one thing or animal into another. Nor is it likely that the druids were rustic philosophers, who debated astronomy and the physical constitution of the earth, as the Classical world did; here is the Noble Savage in another guise, for philosophy was essentially the product of the civilized mind and had no real place in barbarian society. When all the evidence is weighed up, the druids probably were little more than 'witch doctors' to a primitive and undoubtedly very ancient religion. Their beliefs, as far as can be ascertained, lacked any order or over-riding ideology and were concerned with local cults rather than a pantheon of the sort familiar to the Romans/ To use the term druidism implies an elevation of Celtic beliefs that would be unfounded – we might as authoritatively refer to our own society's collection of old wives' tales as a cult. Of the 374 Celtic gods' names known from inscriptions, 305 are known only from one, and only four or five of the rest occur more than 20 times. In his Commentary on the Gallic wars, Caesar tried to equate Celtic with Roman gods, but the results of the exercise are misleading. No fewer than 69 names of Celtic gods have been found coupled with that of Mars in inscriptions from the Celtic lands.

Many of the ancient writers on the Celtic supernatural emphasize the human sacrifice angle of druid lore. Strabo wrote with relish about how human victims were stabbed in the back while the priests made divinations from their death-throes. In case this did not sufficiently disgust his readers, he relates how the druids despatched their human and animal victims by burning them in huge wickerwork cages. Tacitus, on the subject of the British druids, was explicit on the nastier side of their rituals; 'they deemed it indeed a duty to cover their altars with the blood of captives and to consult their deities through human entrails,' he reported. It seems that Celtic indulgence in human sacrifice was something of a by-word in civilized Greek and Roman circles from the third century BC onwards – Dionysius of Halicarnassus, Pomponius Mela and Cicero all refer to it. This is an impressive body of evidence and we cannot ignore it.

Throughout the study of Celtic archaeology the severed head recurs as a *leitmotif*, sometimes in sculpture, sometimes in art, and sometimes in the form of actual skulls from excavations. If any single belief can be claimed to pervade Celtic superstition it is the cult of the severed head; in the head rested everything that made men what they are – it was the seat of the Celtic equivalent of the soul. Because of this factor, head-hunting is a popular subject in Celtic literature, and severed heads appear in Celtic folklore down to the present day, a dim echo of a long tradition. A few examples of the Celtic obsession with heads can be cited from British archaeological sources. Most of the examples come from Romano-British times, suggesting that the Roman pantheon often made little impact on older beliefs. In 1946 three skulls were found, with some Romano-British pottery, between the first and third chambers of Wookey Hole cave, Somerset. Further work between 1947 and 1949 brought to light fourteen more skulls and pottery of Romano-British date but Belgic in form. They were, with one exception, of people between the ages of 25 and 30, of which only two were female. The association of skulls with water is by no means an isolated occurrence. Skulls have a habit of being discovered without their skeletons in Romano-British wells. The famous Romano-British cult well dedicated to the nymph Coventina at Carrawburgh on Hadrian's Wall produced a skull and models of heads. Human skulls were found in a well at Heywood, Wilts, associated with Romano-British pottery and animal bones.

Water figures prominently in Celtic lore, and pools, lochs, rivers and wells were all made the foci of ritual. In later folklore skulls and water were still associated. As is often the case with pagan beliefs, the association has occasionally taken on a Christian guise. Saint Melor, of Cornish and Breton folklore fame, met his end by decapitation and the severed head spoke to the murderer and instructed him to set it on a staff in the ground. When this was done, the skull and staff turned into a beautiful tree, from the root of which an unfailing fountain began to gush. This is the Celticized story of Aaron's Rod.

One modern Scots Gaelic folktale embodies all the essential elements of the pagan Celtic head cult, kept alive down the centuries on the island of Vatersay in the Outer Hebrides, in spite of strong Christian influence. It tells of the murder of three brothers at the 'Well of the Heads', the decapitation of their bodies by their father, and the three prophecies uttered by one of the heads as he passed a prehistoric standing stone. The head told that the living man of which it had been part had made a girl pregnant, and how this baby would grow up to avenge the deaths of its uncles. Just as predicted, when the boy reached fourteen years old he beheaded the murderer and threw the head into a well.

This Vatersay story not only includes the severed head and water elements, but others popular in Celtic lore as well.

Three prophecies were uttered, for three was a magical number to the Celts, and the Dark Age and Medieval Welsh, for example, delighted in making up Triads – groups of three stories or three associated events. It is also notable that the head did not utter its prophecies until a standing stone was reached – could this be because in later Celtic tradition the ancient standing stones of the Bronze Age were still held in respect? It is a point which will be considered later (p. 154).

Talking heads occur elsewhere in Celtic literature. In the Medieval collection of earlier Welsh stories known as the *Mabinogion*, the tale of Branwen tells how the head of her brother Bendigeid Vran was taken to London.

> And Bendigeid Vran commanded them that they should cut off his head. 'And take you my head,' said he, 'and bear it even unto the White Mount in London, and bury it there, with the face towards France. And a long time you will be upon the road. In Harlech you will be feasting seven years, the birds of Rhiannon singing to you the while. And all that time the head will be to you as pleasant company as it ever was when on my body.'

Skulls are not always associated with water cults and wells. Celtic warriors were head-hunters who kept the heads of their enemies as trophies and probably displayed them on the gates of their hillforts. There are a couple of instances of this from Britain. In the excavations at Stanwick in Yorkshire, the Brigantian stronghold, Sir Mortimer Wheeler found an ugly relic of Celtic head-hunting. A skull, bearing three wounds, one of which was fatal, had been detached from the neck below the fourth vertebra. It was clearly the result of a beheading, and had been set up on a pole, or as part of a trophy above the gate. A sword and scabbard discovered nearby may have been part of the ensemble. The skin had still been attached to the skull when it finally fell into the ditch. At Bredon Hill, Gloucestershire, a similar occurrence of skulls displayed above the gate was revealed by the discovery of several during excavations in the 1930s.

There are a few indications of human sacrifice which include the body. The remains of a partly dismembered child were found in excavations of the Iron Age fort at Wandlebury, Cambridge, while at Danebury, Hants, human limbs and torso were discovered in an early Iron Age ritual pit.

A large series of carved stone heads have come to light in Britain and Ireland. The majority are Romano-British in date, and some seem to represent Celtic deities such as Maponus. They are not, however, peculiar to Iron Age and

Roman Britain, but occur in many guises in later superstition. In Yorkshire, the land of the Brigantes who had adorned Stanwick fort with the real article, stone heads seem to have been invested with special properties in local superstition until this century. Twentieth-century stone heads have been carved in a style little different from that employed two millennia ago, and have turned up built into walls of houses and barns, to the confusion of antiquaries. They are rarer elsewhere but evidence suggests that the heads that adorned many medieval churches were more than just amusing ornamental details. They were relics of an older paganism, as frankly barbaric as the Romanesque Whore, who offers herself to visitors to the richly decorated church of SS Mary and David at Kilpeck, Hereford, or the less prominent Lincoln Imp who grins down from a vault in the Cathedral. The power of pagan superstition is long-lived and not easily set aside by reason.

One Romano-British example of a head comes from the Roman fort of Corbridge, just south of Hadrian's Wall, and probably represents the northern god Maponus. A mere 17.8 cm high, its top hollowed to take offerings, it is uncompromisingly awesome. The enormous eyeballs are bulging, but penetrating: the mouth is drawn, the face is triangular.

46 Stone head with horns, Netherby, Cumbria. One of the most dramatic of the large series of carved stone heads of Iron Age and Romano-British date that have been found in Britain. About 18.25 cm high. The ram's horns are perhaps borrowed from Jupiter Ammon, and the sculpture, which can be dated to the second or third century AD, was found in the Roman fort of Castra Exploratum

There is good reason to believe that the religion of the druids goes back a very long way into the mists of prehistory in Europe. There is a growing opinion that Bronze Age Britain was dominated by a priestly caste that was responsible for the great ritual monuments of Avebury, Stonehenge, Brodgar and Callanish. It has even been suggested that this priesthood originated in Neolithic times and that it was responsible for the building of the older henge monuments of the type represented by Durrington Walls in Wiltshire.

Some clues suggest that elements in Celtic religion were rooted much earlier in prehistory. The head cult, for instance, is not peculiar to the Celts, but appears in many societies, including that of Neolithic Britain. Three chalk drums, carved with schematic faces, were found in a child's burial of the very beginning of the Bronze Age, and in style are closely related to representations found in Iberian Neolithic tombs. Dating from somewhat later in the Bronze Age was a stone head discovered in a burial mound at Mecklin Park, Cumberland, while there are several instances in Neolithic chambered tombs of skulls being separated from the rest of the bones, as for example at Wayland's Smithy, Berkshire.

Sometimes earlier religious monuments were re-used in the Iron Age. This is well exemplified by the complex site at Cairnpapple Hill, West Lothian, which may have been one of the major cult centres of Iron Age lowland Scotland. Here a Neolithic henge, a Bronze Age stone circle and a series of later Bronze Age burials were succeeded by a series of Iron Age interments in short stone coffins.

One feature of Iron Age and Romano-British Celtic religion which is certainly of considerable antiquity is the custom of constructing very deep pits or wells into which offerings were thrown. The earliest found is the Wilsford shaft, which dates from the early part of the Bronze Age, and consisted of a shaft, nearly 30.5 m deep and about 1.8 m in diameter. The upper part contained pieces of Bronze Age pottery, and at the bottom there were broken wooden vessels. A Bronze Age shaft discovered at Swanwick, Hants, has elements worthy of a horror-movie: at the bottom was a stake which was packed round with clay. Analysis of a brown deposit on the walls of the lower part of the shaft showed it to have come, in all likelihood, from flesh or blood. Although this cannot be exactly paralleled in Iron Age Britain, this shaft has its almost exact counterpart on the Continent, at Holzhausen in Bavaria. Here excavation inside a rectangular enclosure revealed a pit of almost identical dimensions to that at Swanwick, also containing a stake and traces of blood.

Over a hundred ritual pits and wells, mostly Romano-British but some Iron Age, have been excavated in Britain, and certain types of offerings recur in them. Amongst the most frequent are canine skeletons and skulls (dogs were the attribute of the Celtic mallet god, Sucellos, 'The Good Striker', and of the healing god, Nodens), and bones of hares and cocks, both of which were mentioned by Caesar as being venerated by the Celts. Swords, spears and bars of iron and lead seem to have been bent to 'kill' them as offerings. Iron objects, including knives, and carefully arranged pots, either singly or in groups occur frequently. Now and again other well known attributes of Celtic belief are manifest; hazel nuts, the skulls of ravens, and acorns.

The oak tree was stressed by Classical authors as being particularly venerated by the druids. As Pliny the Elder reported (quoted in B. W. Cunliffe, *Iron Age Communities in Britain*, rev. edn, London, 1978):

> They choose groves of oak for the sake of the tree alone, and they never perform any sacred rite unless they have a branch of it. They think that everything that grows on it has been sent from heaven by the god himself. Mistletoe, however, is rarely found on the oak, and when it is, is gathered with a great deal of ceremony . . . if possible on the sixth day of the moon.

To this account Pliny added that mistletoe was cut with a golden sickle by a white-robed druid after which two bulls were ritually sacrificed. 'They believe that if the mistletoe is taken as a drink, it makes barren animals fertile, and is a remedy against all poison.' In view of its poisonous reputation, no doubt it distracted the imbiber wonderfully from his previous discomfort.

Some pits contained complete human skeletons. In one found at Greenhithe, Kent, three had been placed side by side at the bottom. In one of the many ritual pits found at the site of the Roman forts at Newstead, a skeleton was 'standing' upright with a spear nearby. Another pit contained the skeleton of a dwarf.

An old Irish story tells how the Celtic god known as the Dagda (the Good God) attended a feast prepared for him, in which a porridge of four score gallons of fresh milk, a similar amount of meal and fat, goats, pigs and sheep, was boiled up and poured into a hole in the ground. 'Then the Dagda took his ladle, and it was big enough for a man and a woman to lie in the middle of it' and ate the concoction out of the pit.

Most places sacred to the Celts were unmarked by structures – pools, springs, wells, lochs, groves, clearings, rocks or individual trees leave little for archaeologists – but a few more permanent remains have been found. A rectangular wooden temple was discovered to have stood at Heathrow, Middlesex, from the fourth century BC onwards. It displays a close similarity to later Romano-Celtic temples, with a central shrine set within a rectangular ambulatory, the entire structure covering little more than 2.8 sq. m. A comparable temple was found inside the Iron Age fort at South Cadbury, Somerset. This too was rectan-

47 Wooden figure from Dagenham, Essex, 48.5 cm high. Although undatable, the style of this carving suggests it is of the early Iron Age, and it can be compared with a series of wooden figures found at the source of the Seine. It is certainly prehistoric, for it is made of pinewood, and pine became extinct in England at an early date. It has a hole for the attachment of a separate penis

gular but had a small porch and no ambulatory. It was approached through a complex of ritual pits containing animal burials. At Maiden Castle, on the other hand, the temple plan was circular and differed little from an Iron Age house. A Romano-British temple had been built on top of it, and a burial of an infant had been made just outside the door. At Frilford, Berkshire, a Romano-British temple overlay an earlier shrine. This was set within a penannular ditched enclosure, very reminiscent of a Neolithic henge monument, and perhaps in the light of modern arguments (p. 153) can be seen as the descendant of one. Nearby a second Romano-British temple overlay a circular enclosure

48 Head of a shield-carrying warrior from a group of wooden figures in a ship found at Roos Carr. Height of head: *c*.5 cm. The group (which originally comprised five figures) was found in the Humber estuary in 1836. Arguments have again surrounded its date – it has been claimed as late Bronze Age on account of the round shields carried by the warriors, and Viking on account of the animal prow of the ship. But round shields were also carried in the Iron Age, and animal prows are depicted on a ship shown on an Iron Age coin, so it is as likely to be Iron Age as late Bronze Age. A Viking date is most improbable

delimited by timber posts, in which were two child burials. Among the finds were models of a Celtic shield and sword, and an iron ploughshare had been deposited in a ritual pit. Other votive model shields have been found in Britain at Hod Hill, Dorset, and Worth, Kent. Circular ditched shrines have also been discovered at Winchester and Brigstock, Northants.

Few Iron Age representations that are certainly of deities can be recognized from Britain. Wooden carvings of probable but uncertain Iron Age date have been found in various parts of the country; there is one from Dagenham, Essex, and another from Teingrace, Devon, for example. What conclusions are to be made of the Ballachulish Image, the starkly sexual effigy of a woman that was found in a peat bog in 1880 in Argyllshire? On exposure to the air it warped and twisted, but it is still an object of some impact on the observer. Even more evocative to the eye attuned to the simpler geometry of modern sculpture are the five warriors found at Roos Carr on the Humber, standing with round shields in a boat with dragon prow. The Viking appearance of their ship has led some to suggest a Dark Age date for them, but a dragon prow appears on a ship illustrated on an Iron Age Armorican coin, so there is no reason to insist that they are not Iron Age. With pebble eyes and slit mouths, they are malignant and menacing images from the pre-historic unconscious of the European mind.

The climax of Iron Age Britain

It was the Belgae, hailing from an area to the south of modern Belgium, who were the catalyst in the last chaotic and tumultuous century of Iron Age Celtic Britain.

This was an age when the Celtic British tribes were almost too barbarian to be true. The Celtic spirit rose to excesses in petty quarrels and warfare, in the production of garish metalwork and ornaments (pp. 72f.), and in lavish and complex fort defences (p. 56). Scholars today disagree over the exact tribes which enjoyed and endured Belgic aristo-cratic overlordship, but there is no doubt that the influence of the Belgae was a minor rival to that of Rome. The tribes that came under Belgic influence were more advanced than their neighbours – they developed the cultural side of life and engaged in a hearty political intercourse that has been traced through the coins that they hoarded or inadvertently dropped.

The period began unremarkably enough with the infiltra-tion of newcomers from the Continent, known only from a few stray finds and historical sources. It ended in the full spotlight of history, dominated by personalities whose characters remain forceful after two millennia: Commius of the Atrebates, Cassivellaunus of the Catuvellauni, and the great Cunobelin, immortalized as Cymbeline by Shake-speare.

Archaeological evidence suggests that, oddly enough, the Belgae were not thoroughbred Celts. They seem to have had some admixture of Germanic blood before they left their homeland and settled in Britain. Much of the evidence

(a)

49 Celtic British coins. All enlarged.

(a) Gallo-Belgic 'A' stater, brought to Britain by Belgic immigrants at the end of the second or early in the first century BC. The ultimate model for the design is a Greek coin of Philip of Macedon – the obverse represents 'Apollo', the reverse a chariot. Gold. From a cast of a coin in the British Museum

(b) Gallo-Belgic 'E' gold stater. Such coins were brought to Britain by immigrants trying to flee from Caesar around 57 BC. On the obverse the head of Apollo has been so defaced that the design is totally obliterated, and the 'chariot' on the reverse is a dismembered horse, which can be compared with the Uffington White Horse (Plate 20). (Heberden Coin Room, Ashmolean Museum)

(c) Gold stater of British 'triple-tailed horse' type. The model is still a coin of Philip of Macedon, the chariot now a wheel beneath the horse on the reverse. This coin was probably struck between about 40 and 20 BC, and was current over a wide area in southern England. It served as a model for the later coins of the Dobunni, and for the issues of Commius of the Atrebates. Sometimes termed 'British Q'. (From a cast of a coin in the British Museum)

(b)

(c)

surrounding the early settlements of the Belgae is ambiguous, provided by coins that are notoriously difficult to evaluate, and by slight references in the pages of Caesar. Consequently the exact date of the first settlement is in dispute – it could be as early as 150 BC, though the least disputable evidence is almost a century later than this.

Apart from their coins, very few objects made before about 50 BC can be attributed to the Belgae: they used the same pots, houses and metalwork as the indigenous population, and made no innovations that have survived. After this period, however, several distinctive features can be determined archaeologically. The Aylesford-Swarling cemeteries (p.140) produced objects which can be matched with some on the Continent. Since these objects have been

(d)

(e)

(f)

(d) Silver coin of Eppillus of the Atrebates (c.AD 5–10). Struck at Calleva (Silchester), this coin shows Roman influence in its design. Eppillus was one of the successors of Commius. From a cast of a coin in the British Museum

(e) Gold stater of Cunobelin, struck at Colchester. Roman influence is apparent in the design, and the ear of barley on the obverse may be an answer to the vine-leaf that appears on some coins of Verica (Plate 7c), a nationalistic 'British beer is better than Roman wine', perhaps? (Ashmolean Museum)

(f) Cast bronze coin of the Durotriges. Known as 'Hengistbury Head' coins on account of a large hoard found at this site in Dorset, they represent the final degeneration of the Apollo/chariot design. They were current around the time of the Claudian invasion. From a cast of a coin in the British Museum

found with Roman merchandise of known date, they can by inference be assigned to around the last half of the first century BC.

Thus can archaeology produce evidence to support at least part of Caesar's assertion that 'the coast [of Britain] is inhabited by Belgic immigrants who came over to plunder and make wars, nearly all of them retaining the names of the tribes from which they originated, and later settled down to till the soil' (Caesar, *The Conquest of Gaul,* trans. S. A. Handford, Harmondsworth, 1951). It is clear that people came from Belgic areas on the Continent, bringing their own coins and, by 50 BC if not before, producing objects distinctively their own. The rest of Caesar's statement is less easily substantiated, since it suggests that there was a piecemeal

91

entrance, not one migration, probably a series of Belgic cross-Channel movements at some date prior to that at which Caesar was writing.

To this can be added another statement of Caesar (op. cit.): 'Divitiacus, the most powerful king of Gaul, controlled not only a large part of the Belgic territory but Britain as well . . . within living memory.' This implies that Belgic rule had been established at least a generation before Caesar's time: well before archaeological evidence can be found.

It is at this point that coins become vital evidence. Their use of coins at once sets the Belgae apart from the more traditionally rooted British Celts. Coins, based on classical forms, show that the Belgae possessed a primitive money economy, or a flourishing trade. More importantly, they show that the Belgic peoples, barbarians from their helmets down to their feet, were acting a new Innocent – this time in a seduction scene with the libertine called Civilization. The first Belgic coin was minted on the Continent, and by the time the tribes had reached Britain Gallo-Belgic coinage was well-developed. The coins turn up in the Thames basin, Kent and Essex, as incriminatingly as champagne corks.

Coins are important historically because they are usually closely datable. Some of those produced by Rome were so inscribed that the information can be translated into an exact month and year of minting. Thus coins are helpful in putting rough dates to objects found in association with them. But what is to be made of Belgic coins? How can these discs of gold be used to achieve dating evidence for the first Belgic intruders in Britain? There are no inscriptions on them until very nearly the end of the first century BC, no consuls or emperors or events commemorated. Sometimes only a badly drawn head of Apollo copied from numerous copies of a Macedonian original is faintly recognizable. Some degenerate into blobs and whirls that started life in superb classical symmetry, others retain some clarity. The truth is, before about 60 BC the dating of Belgic coinage in Britain is far from certain, and even the date usually now accepted for the earliest Belgic coins in England (in the late second century BC) is not founded on irrefutable logic.

After about 50 BC, however, the dating of coins becomes more certain, and it is often possible to assign a particular piece to a generation if not a decade with some degree of certainty. It is thus not until the historical sources become fairly common and archaeological evidence for the Belgae more clear-cut that the coins are sufficiently inscribed to yield at least the names of a few Belgic leaders.

One certain fact stands out in the confusion of Belgic history: Julius Caesar fragmented the course of events in Britain. In 55 BC he dealt the Celts a historic blow that shattered their cultural development for five centuries. The reconnaissance trip he made in that year, followed by the full-scale invasion in 54 BC, can be reduced to fairly minor events in terms of Roman imperial development, but they had far-reaching effects on the Celts. Caesar arrived at precisely the point when the Belgic kingdoms had formed and were engaged in complex political dealings.

The first of the heroic figures of Belgic Britain was integral to Caesar's schemes for conquest. This man was Commius, king of the Continental Belgic tribe of the Atrebates, who had been given his status by the Romans themselves. Commius had contacts with Britain – one section of the Atrebates had already established themselves in southern England. What happened on the Continent was not only a matter of personal interest to men whose families still lived abroad, but also of political urgency. The Continental Celts had seen Caesar and the Roman legions move northwards into Gaul and build lighthouses, forts and towns. On a good day the British Celts could stand on the White Cliffs of Dover and see the Roman Empire a mere 35 km and a few hours' sail by military transport away. It was not surprising that many southerners felt it expedient to throw in their hand to help the losing side by shipping men, supplies and treasures across the Channel and by providing asylum on the South Downs for the wounded or dispirited. According to Caesar the druids were an active force behind these subversive actions.

The Celts reacted to Caesar's impending visit with characteristic confusion. Tribal politics were complicated, and if the Britons had the psychological advantage of never having played host to Rome before, they still apparently underestimated the dangers. To some tribes the advantages of allegiance to Rome held very clear short- and long-term benefits. It has recently been demonstrated that Caesar lacked senatorial authority for carrying out a conquest in 55 BC. He was almost certainly arriving not as a conqueror, but partly to wipe out the British helpers of his Continental foes, and partly to test Roman public opinion. Modern scholarship has only just revealed this, but the British tribes, in close contact with the Continent at the time, must surely have been aware of it. They could not have foreseen that the initial successes of the sortie to Britain could have resulted in resounding senatorial approval and authority the following year for the conquest proper. Perhaps they listened too closely to the blandishments of Commius, who had been sent ahead of the legions to persuade the tribes to acquiesce. The complexities must elude us now, but it is evident that the whole truth is not to be found in the writings of Caesar. Commius was arrested on his arrival in Britain, but quickly released when the Romans landed. Yet in 54 BC, when the Romans finally cornered Cassivellaunus of the Catuvellauni in Wheathampstead, it was Commius who was used as an envoy, and whose mediation brought about the rather overdue peace treaty. This event would probably not have taken place had not Mandubracius, prince of the Trinovantes, fled to Caesar asking for help against Catuvellaunian aggression.

Of the many tribal groups that crystallized themselves around the time of Caesar, the Catuvellauni were dominant. Though they had acquired many of the attributes of a Belgic way of life they were in effect only first-generation Belgae. They hailed from the Marne, and were relative newcomers who, like many of their kind, pretended that they were long-established and proud of their native ancestry. The homeland of the Catuvellauni lay north of London. After Caesar had left their role was paramount.

The legions left with promises to shield the Trinovantes from Catuvellaunian aggression, and there was a power-shuffle in Britain. The people of Kent, who in the time of Divitiacus had probably been among the most prosperous, opposed Caesar and accordingly felt the draught. The Trinovantes, however, began trading vigorously with the Roman World, and Trinovantian chiefs were soon tippling the best Falernian wine from Roman tableware.

In the 90 years following 54 BC, despite the treaties with Rome, a power struggle ensued between Trinovantes and Catuvellauni. Briefly, the Catuvellauni enjoyed supremacy under their leader Tasciovanus, but on his death the kingdom broke up. A late contemporary of Tasciovanus was Cunobelin. His origins are obscure, but he rapidly rose on the death of Tasciovanus around AD 10 to a position of strength, ruling both Catuvellauni and Trinovantes in a new expanded kingdom until just before the invasion of Britain by the emperor Claudius in AD 43. Cunobelin was described by the Roman writer Suetonius as 'king of Britain', and he was the only pre-Roman chief to enjoy the distinction of being remembered in later times. Cunobelin's court was no barbarian pigsty. He enjoyed Roman luxuries, and there is good reason to believe that some of his followers could read and write Latin.

To the west of the pro-Roman cultural bloc lay other warring tribes. In Hampshire, centred on Silchester, were the Atrebates. For some reason unknown to history, their kinsman Commius had eventually fled from Caesar and come to Britain where he presumably became king. Despite these beginnings, the Atrebates became increasingly pro-Roman, a fact which led to their estrangement from their western neighbours, the Dobunni. The Dobunni had entered into no Roman alliances, though they were not averse, as finds from their capital at Bagendon near Cirencester show, to some good Roman wine and Roman-style pottery imported from Gaul.

Augustus envisaged completion of his adopted father's work by annexing Britain for the Roman Empire. To this end he fostered trade between Britain and the Roman world, and encouraged pro-Roman tendencies. But he died with his task unaccomplished, and the emperor Caligula's mission to Britain in AD 41 ended farcically with his soldiers collecting shells on the Gaulish coast of the Channel. It was not until the emperor Claudius' reign that political events played again into Roman hands.

The Romanization of Belgic Britain

After Caesar's expeditions, trade between Celtic Britain and the Roman world increased – particularly from 15 BC onwards. Around 50 BC a few bronze vessels and amphorae of luxury wine arrived, but by 15 BC rough wines were imported for a less discriminating market. By the last decade of the first century BC amphorae were also coming in, filled with products such as fish-sauce from the southern Spanish coastal region. More durable luxuries came too. Of these, the most notable were different types of tableware. The finest was Arretine pottery – fine red-gloss ware produced in the Arezzo area of Italy and often richly decorated in relief with classical compositions and motifs. Arretine was still imported to Britain after the Claudian conquest, when it had ceased to be used by the military of the German frontier forts. This was probably because of sharp practice on the part of the merchants who were unloading old stock on an eager but undiscriminating market. The phenomenon can be seen on several occasions in Britain of the first century AD – in East Anglia people were happily using styles of pottery 50 years after they had ceased to be fashionable elsewhere, and which represent old stock rather than new pots in old styles.

The main imports, however, were the products of the Gallo-Belgic pottery industry. This had grown up to serve

95

the markets of northern Gaul, and produced cheap imitations of the better-class wares. The story is a familiar one to modern ears. Enterprising potters in southern Gaul found they could make passable copies of Arretine, and copies of this down-market pottery (known as south Gaulish Samian) had a ready market in the north. The best was *Terra Rubra*, a red-slip ware which attempted to imitate the superior red-gloss wares of Arezzo and southern Gaul. Not as blatant was *Terra Nigra*, a Continental black-slip ware in similar shapes (platters were the most popular) which ousted *Terra Rubra* in popularity at British feasts. Not to be outdone, the British attempted their own versions. *Terra Rubra* was produced in the neighbourhood of Colchester, with a feeble red slip and no pretence at a gloss. British *Terra Nigra* may have been produced at other centres as well, and spawned its own imitations which survived long enough to be taken by the Roman army into Scotland. The volume of trade in Gallo-Belgic pottery was considerable. About a hundred sites all over the Belgic areas of Britain have produced some, and while the largest assemblages come not unexpectedly from major centres such as Colchester, Silchester and Bagendon, the appearance of Gallo-Belgic sherds on otherwise minor sites shows that the trade was far-reaching and the products did not grace only the noblest tables. Romanized culture had begun to permeate all sections of society.

The pottery trade was supplemented by a lesser traffic in Roman jugs and flagons, no doubt for the decanting of wine. There was too a specialist trade in items which only the richest could afford. Silver cups, produced in the Campanian area of Italy, found their way into chieftains' burials

50 Silver cup of the first century BC, made probably in Italy and imported to adorn a Belgic chieftain's feast in Britain. It came from a richly furnished grave at Welwyn, Hertfordshire, excavated in 1906

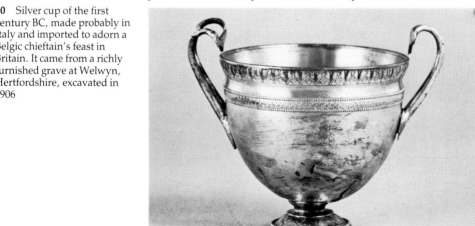

at Welwyn, Herts. Apart from the silverwork, there were other vessels of bronze and glass, known from chieftains' burials, and even the occasional work of art. The impressive bronze bust of the emperor Caligula, mounted on its pedestal, that was found in Colchester, was almost certainly a pre-Conquest import, while the bronze figurines of a stag and a boar from the Lexden tumulus just outside the same city were undoubtedly brought from Gaul shortly before the arrival of Claudius.

Roman influence appeared in more subtle guises, for instance in coinage. Roman Republican coins found their way to Britain in small numbers after the Caesarian expeditions. It is very unlikely that any served as currency; they were probably used as ornaments. A pendant found in the Lexden tumulus had been made from a denarius of Augustus, struck in 17 BC, the portrait of the emperor having been carefully cut from the coin. A hint, however, that a few coins may have seen limited circulation comes from Colchester, where excavations on the Sheepen site brought to light a British imitation of a Roman denarius, not exactly copying any known Roman coin but quite similar to one of Titus Carisius, a moneyer operating in Rome around 45 BC.

51 Group of bronze objects from a chieftain's burial at Lexden, just outside Colchester, and datable to the eve of the Claudian invasion. The objects include three bronzes (a boar, an ox and a putto), a pendant made out of a coin of Augustus (foreground, see Plate 52), a griffin, a wreath (at the rear of the picture) and various mounts and studs. The grave also contained amphorae (wine storage vessels) and other pots, chain mail, and a bronze table

The native British coinage became progressively influenced by Roman designs in the early years of the first century AD. Many of the latest issues of south-east England are so close to the official Roman style that it seems probable that Roman engravers (or Celtic die sinkers trained in Roman workshops) were producing the designs. If these were simply slavish copies of Roman designs, or Romanized interpretations of Celtic types, they might be regarded as the product of a curious but superficial fashion. But they are not.

52 Pendant made out of a denarius of Augustus, from the Lexden Grave

The latest issues of the Belgic dynasties before the Claudian invasion boast a variety of types, many of which seem to be Celtic interpretations of Roman themes executed to suit Romanized taste. The purpose of such 'Romanizing' coins could well have been that they were intended for Roman coffers, either as trade payments or the tribute money due under Caesar's treaties.

The first 'Romanizing' coins appear to have been struck around 15 BC, and were issued by Tincommius of the Atrebates and Tasciovanus of the Catuvellauni. This date coincides remarkably with the sudden increase in Roman and Romanized imports, and with Augustus' sudden interest in the island. Horace, in one of his Odes written around this time, includes the Britons in his list of admirers of Augustus, and it is noticeable how often portraits of Augustus, sometimes thinly disguised, appear on Celtic

British coins. The Atrebates continued their contacts with Rome – Tincommius' father was almost certainly the Commius Caesar knew, and his successors, Verica and Eppillus, carried the pro-Roman policy into coinage. Verica even struck a coin with a vine leaf as an obverse type, perhaps an allusion to the wine trade, and which has been seen as a challenge to the ear of barley (representing British beer?) that made its appearance on coins of Cunobelin around the same time.

(a)

(b)

53 Celtic British coins showing Roman influence. (a) A silver issue of Tincommius with a charging bull on the reverse and Apollo on the obverse, modelled on a Roman denarius struck by Augustus at Lyons between 15 and 12 BC. (b) A bronze coin of Cunobelin, the obverse of which is modelled on a portrait of Augustus. The reverse is a very classical subject – a centaur blowing a horn – but it is not directly copied from a Roman coin, and the horn may be native. From casts of coins in the British Museum

On the coins of Eppillus and Verica appear a Latin title – *Rex*. The title, which meant simply 'king', is one which had been held in contempt in the Roman world for five centuries since the death of the last king of Rome, Tarquinius Superbus. It had no contemptible overtones in the barbarians' minds, and Roman diplomacy bestowed the title when and as it was felt politic. It is not known whether Tincommius and Verica assumed the title or whether it was awarded them for their support of Rome – the title was also used by Cunobelin. Either way, its use betokens a respect for Rome and for Roman ways, and implies Roman influence in the chieftains' courts.

Even more significant is the implication of literacy suggested by the inscriptions in Latin letters that appear on the coins. The first inscriptions on Belgic coins appeared in the time of Commius himself. He figures shortly before

25 BC as COMMIOS. Only slightly later are the inscribed issues of Tasciovanus of the Catuvellauni, whose lettering closely resembles that of Commius and his successor Tincommius. For the most part the inscriptions are confined to the names of chiefs or to mints. Some puzzling inscriptions, usually taken to be personal names, may have been abbreviated titles, or may have held some other significance now lost. What is to be made of such legends as ALE SCA or ESVP ASV on Coritanian coins, or even the mysterious RVIIS on coins struck by Tasciovanus? In virtually all the inscriptions the lettering is good, which implies a degree of literacy on the part of the engraver. Somewhat earlier, around the beginning of the first century BC, there is evidence that papyrus was being imported to Britain and used for making moulds for casting coins. It is hardly likely that papyrus was imported primarily for this purpose, and its presence in Britain implies some kind of literacy even before the time of Caesar. Graffiti occur on pottery at Colchester before the Conquest – and consist of abbreviated names. They appear only on the very best pottery, as might be expected, and might in some cases have been the work of Continentals staying in Colchester in Cunobelin's court. Some British *Terra Nigra* carries maker's stamps, usually blundered, but in a few cases suggestive that the manufacturers recognized the letters they were using.

By the first century Britain knew all about the Roman way of life. In AD 43 she was to be sharply reminded of the Roman way of death.

The Roman Interlude Chapter three

In the British Museum there is a Roman marble head, a mere 29.2 cm high, in almost perfect condition, which was dredged up from Bosham Harbour, Sussex, in 1910. It is a purely Classical sculpture with finely executed features and a realism that shows it to be a portrait. Everything about it is Classical – no Celtic workshop could have produced such an object. Yet it is an enigma of Celtic Britain. If we discount the possibility that it was lost overboard at the end of some Grand Tour, its presence in British waters is of great curiosity. Sculptural studies suggest that it is the portrait of a member of the Imperial family – almost certainly Germanicus. It seems inconceivable that a work of art with these intimate connections with the Emperor's family should have been imported before the Roman conquest. It seems equally surprising that it should have been brought in after the conquest – at least 24 years after Germanicus' death.

The most likely explanation is that it was on its way to an early Imperial shrine, or to a great house in the area. The nearby discovery of a unique palace at Fishbourne – the most splendid stately home to have left traces from the Roman period – seems to settle the matter of its intended destination.

The head and its conjectural history highlight the change that came over southern Britain as soon as the legions arrived intent on conquest in AD 43. Fishbourne and Bosham harbour lie in the centre of Atrebatan territory, and it was in this area that an early Roman supply base has been discovered. The Atrebates had obviously continued their long association with Rome and their support was of vital importance in the success of the conquest. They were Celts, but they were Belgae too, and it fell to their destiny to effect the final civilization of their people. The area grew rapidly in prosperity and it is not by chance that Fishbourne with its 49 ha of magnificently furnished public and private rooms belonged almost certainly not to some Roman official but to the king of the southern Atrebates (by this time known as the Regnenses), Cogidubnus.

Cogidubnus was an important figure in British-Roman

relations. He had the Roman title *Rex* and was without a doubt a man of highly developed Roman tastes.

The Bosham head and its history illuminate too some of the problems besetting students of the Celts under Roman rule. Historical sources for the period are more abundant than in the preceding era and more reliable than in that succeeding. We know the names of the emperors, many generals and administrators, some of the doctors, potters and even more humble folk such as the actress and the gladiator who scratched their names on a Leicester potsherd. There are inscriptions on everyday objects, on buildings, on walls. On the other hand the artefacts do not always tell the same story as the written sources. There is also the difficulty of the differing attitudes of the Celts to Rome: some reacted with ferocity, others like Cogidubnus were eager to throw in their lot with the Empire. They quickly became Romanized – indeed they eventually retained some aspects of Roman life that had long since gone out of fashion on the Continent. They are therefore indistinguishable from longer-established citizens by the things they left behind them. Their story belongs to that of Roman Britain: *Romanitas* followed the advance of the legions to the frontier of Hadrian's Wall. This boundary fluctuated in the second century – sometimes the Celts as far north as the Antonine Wall were incorporated into the Empire, at other times they were free, but, effectively, the areas south of this wide border area were Romano-British for four centuries. After 212 or 214, all those people living within the Imperial boundaries were decreed citizens and the exercise to distinguish Celt from Roman became meaningless. From 43 onwards, Celts who happened to be living in the southern parts of Britannia congregated in towns, joined the army, learned to speak Latin, abandoned their traditional roles in life and took up new skills and pastimes. The Celts in the southern areas that were not still under military control (the Civil Zone) were Romans.

Even Roman civilization could not eradicate a millennium of development, however. The Celts under Roman rule retained certain aspects of the traditions, though most were sublimated until the legions had left. Perhaps the most significant factor was that the tribal structure was not disrupted. As the Romans demolished the hillforts, they resettled the population in towns that became tribal capitals. Thus, to take just one example, Cirencester was Corinium Dobunnorum, the capital of the Dobunni tribe. From the late first century on, however, the Celtic spirit was diverted into civilized effort.

In such areas as art, where clear attempts to mix the two cultures can be seen, there is an important distinction to be made; after the Roman conquest the Celts were actively trying to cater for Roman tastes, whereas their Iron Age predecessors had been more passive receptacles of Classical culture. After the initial impact of the conquest Celtic art took the severe naturalism of Classical art in its stride and began to soften it. At first the two traditions made uneasy bedfellows, as can be demonstrated by the decoration on the

54 Bronze mount, perhaps for a box, from Elmswell, Yorkshire. This mount combines both Celtic and Roman features. The enamel ivyscroll is purely Roman, as is the symmetry of the lyrescroll beneath, but lyrescroll and 'berried rosette' are both features of Belgic art at the beginning of the first century AD. Late first century AD. Width: 24 cm

bronze mount for a box from Elmswell, Northants, of the later first century. Here Celtic lyre-scroll and berried rosette (a development of the post-conquest Celts) is juxtaposed with an enamelled band of Roman ivyscroll. By the second century the initial difficulties had been overcome, as evidenced by a series of brooches Roman in design but Celtic in taste. On the superb gold fan-tailed brooch from Greatchesters (Aesica) on Hadrian's Wall two Celtic creatures (or are they merely trumpet patterns?) confront each other in a composition wholly Classical in its symmetry, wholly Celtic in its inspiration. Classical dolphins provide the stimulus for mounts for pony harnesses on the late first-century find from Polden Hill, Somerset, while sea-horses (hippocamps) are given Celtic guise on the dragonesque fibulae-brooches produced to suit Celtic taste on the northern frontier of second-century Britannia. The list of Classical borrowings in Celtic-style art is long and can be matched by Celtic influences on Classical-style art. The bronze head of a girl found at Silkstead has Celtic eyes vacantly staring from a Classically realistic face; the podgy Venus in the mosaic from Rudston dreams of her Cocidius rather than her Mars.

One category of the artist's work that should be considered are the so-called Celtic heads (p. 83) of which the majority come from Romano-British contexts. Most of these are crude and stylized, the work of artists unfamiliar with their medium and the message. Some are obviously attempting Classical subjects, though with notable rudeness, while others seem to ignore anything but the simplest symbolism in their aims. They seem to speak not of the Celtic present, but of the Celtic past.

A close scrutiny of the artefacts or the buildings, then, yields very little information about the surviving culture of the Celts as they adopted Roman ways. One of the great drawbacks of archaeological evidence is that it says nothing about custom, superstitions, folklore or language, the very

55 Hollow bronze head of a girl, Silkstead, Hampshire. This is a Romano-British work, with typically 'Celtic' formal almond-shaped eyes, coarse hair and disregard for portraiture, combined with 'Roman' features such as the plump face, carefully modelled skull and mouth. The eyes are black pebbles. First or second century AD. Height: c.12.5 cm

substance of folk culture. It cannot be disputed for instance that Hebridean crofters maintain today an ancient Celtic culture with folktales and customs that originated in the Middle Ages and possible long before in the Iron Age. Yet archaeologically this vigorous culture will leave no trace. By the same token it is impossible to tell whether the inhabitants of Viroconium (Wroxeter) continued to celebrate Celtic festivals, sing Celtic songs and tell their children Celtic stories. All we can do is infer that the changeover was fairly slow until a distinctively Romano-British culture had evolved.

The resistance fighters
Outside the Roman areas, in the north particularly, the Empire had little effect on the native population. The archaeological material shows no break – pottery, houses and general way of life were unchanged. Border areas seem to have been affected by Roman doctrine which permeated into the Dark Ages, but apart from the physical barrier of Hadrian's Wall which probably prevented the traditional movement of stock, Celts were still Celts in the north. In

areas where the Romans found little politically or econo-
mically to exploit (such as Wales or Cornwall) Romanization
of everyday life was rare, imports sparse and only the ethos
of Rome lived on into the Dark Ages.

Only a few historical tales and some burnt layers in
excavations are testimony to the heroism of those Celts who
viewed the Roman advance with dismay. A few characters
are prominent – Boudicca and Caratacus perhaps the most
famous. As time progressed, however, the urgency of Celtic
causes lessened. The motives for rebellion became more
political than chauvinistic. There were even several attempts
to set up separate Empires in Britannia, and at least one of
the leaders was of Celtic (though Continental) origin.
These cannot be claimed as Celtic uprisings – political
quarrels with the Empire were the main driving force and
archaeologically there is nothing to distinguish these phases
from the rest of the Roman period.

. It fell to the limping, stammering emperor Claudius to
seal the fate of the British Celts. Raised to the purple partly
because of his lack of presence, he could hardly have
differed more from the great British king of the period,
Cunobelin of the Catuvellauni. For years the strength and
force of this Celtic leader had kept the Britons free from
Roman intervention, and at the same time the Catuvellauni
had been steadily encroaching on their neighbours despite
the treaties agreed when Caesar left.

In AD 41 the south of Britain was relatively stable. Then
Cunobelin died. His successors Togodubnus and Caratacus
(known to history as his sons though now thought not to
have been so closely related) began a struggle for supremacy
that led eventually in AD 42 to Verica of the Atrebates
fleeing to the emperor of Rome. He pleaded for help and the
political and personal gains did not fail to occur to the
Romans. Here, said Rome officially, was the trusty ally
being humiliated and driven out of his rightful lands. Here
too, she added aside, was a potential province, already open
to civilized suggestion and well known to abound in
hunting dogs, pearls, gold, wheat, hides, timber and slaves.

Accordingly, over 20,000 legionaries and as many lesser
ranks bobbed their way across the Channel, and this time
made a base camp at Richborough. As Dr Johnson once
remarked of a man about to be hanged, the thought of death
concentrates the mind wonderfully. So too, it might be
added, does it patch up old squabbles. Togodubnus and
Caratacus joined forces, mustered all their resources
behind the Medway, rallied the fighting spirit of the Celts
and were totally beaten. Claudius accompanied his vic-

torious army to capture Colchester, Togodubnus died in battle and Caratacus fled to stir up the Silures in south Wales.

During the next few years the Celts were almost helpless victims of Rome, despite their determined efforts to resist. Hillfort after hillfort in the south fell to the ruthless charge of the future emperor Vespasian, tribe after tribe gave in, accepted rehabilitation in the new towns and contented themselves with listening to stories of the fighting in Wales in the 60s and in Scotland in the following decades.

In 59 Suetonius Paulinus began to extend Roman control into north Wales, and by 61 the chief trouble spot was Anglesey, a hotbed of Celtic fervour and the stronghold of the druids. Tacitus described the confrontation of Roman and druids thus: 'The front battle line stood on the opposite shore in a dense mass, women running among them, their hair dishevelled like the Furies, bringing forward torches. Round about stood Druids, raising their hands to the sky and uttering terrible curses.' Eventually the daunted soldiers rallied and Anglesey fell. Tersely Tacitus records that the Romans 'destroyed the groves devoted to Mona's barbarous superstitions'. The votive offerings found accidentally in the Llyn Cerrig Bach lake (pp. 19–20) are evidence of these rites, and from now on the Celts had lost one of the most important facets of their life. Religious strength was sapped, and the druids were ghosts of the past. Much of what was traditionally Celtic died with them. Religion was diverted into adopting Roman gods – Sulis-Minerva at Bath is a famous example of Romano-Celtic religious amalgamation. The world of the Iron Age Celts was fading away.

With the fall of Anglesey, Wales had technically been conquered, though the consolidation of victory was not achieved for some decades. In 61, however, a second blow to Romano-Celtic relations was dealt. It was the culmination of several years of unrest, in which the pro-Roman queen Cartimandua (of the Brigantes, or possibly the Coritani) had played an important part. Her Romanophile politics had led to the final personal defeat of Caratacus, whose campaigns in south Wales had resulted in his fleeing to the queen. Promptly she had handed him over to the Romans. Cartimandua's policies were not shared by her husband Venutius, who carried on the fight for independence from his base at Stanwick, Yorks.

In about 60, too, the king of Iceni, Prasutagus, died, leaving his estate jointly to his two daughters and the Empire – a common arrangement that was calculated to

allow his family to retain at least some of his lands.
However, the Roman administrators overstepped their
mark, and treated Boudicca and her daughters with a
marked lack of respect. Personal enmity grew, Boudicca
resisted, her daughters were raped and she herself flogged.
The queen made reprisals and 70,000 lives were lost.

Three cities, Colchester, St Albans and London were
razed. The historian Tacitus described the scene in
Colchester thus:

> While things were in this state of turmoil, the statue of Victory at
> Colchester fell down without any visible cause, and in falling
> turned face down, as if yielding to the enemy. Several women in
> a state of frenzy prophesied of the impending destruction, and
> proclaimed that the voices of barbarians had been heard in the
> council chamber, that howling had echoed round the theatre,
> that an apparition of the overthrown *colonia* had been seen in the
> sea [i.e. the Thames Estuary]. The sea appeared like blood, and in
> the ebb the ghosts of human corpses were left behind on the
> shore.

The legions retaliated with a loss of a further 80,000 Celtic
lives. The acting commander of the second legion, who had
refused to send help in the first troubles, heard of the
bloodshed and fell on his sword. The revolt of Boudicca,
Celtic Britain's most famous lady, ended in tragedy.

In the north, however, the Celts still resisted. Venutius'
stand lasted but a short time. In the end the Brigantes south
of Hadrian's Wall, while never fully Romanized and always
ready to revolt, were forced into an uneasy peace. It is
notable that the frontier work is as well defended against
attack from the south as from the north. The constant
changes in frontier policy reflect the continuing problems of
the Celtic tribes until the last days of Roman Britain.

By 79, the conquest of what is now southern Scotland was
under way. The commander in charge, Agricola, was the
son-in-law of Tacitus the historian, so there is a fairly full
account of the events. He established a line of forts which
was later replaced by Hadrian's Wall. In 84 Agricola put to
flight 30,000 Caledonian Celts in the battle of Mons
Graupius – the whereabouts of which is unknown, though
it could be Duncrub, Perthshire. The aim of Hadrian's Wall,
put up in the years following 122, was not merely to prevent
Celts from moving into the Empire and causing trouble; it
was a symbolic edge to the Empire. It certainly did not
prevent the Celts from uprising, and within twenty years a
second Wall was constructed further north – testimony to
the failure of the first. This too did not prove too great an
obstacle for the Celtic tribes, and the archaeological
evidence for the period is of forts razed or abandoned,

refurbished or rebuilt as the politics and local relations dictated.

With such bloodshed did Celtic Britain become Roman Britannia, but even as the metamorphosis was taking place other barbarians were challenging the might of civilization.

The barbarian infiltrators

In the second century, barbarian pressure started to build up on the frontiers of the Empire – Rome had conquered more than she could easily hold. From this period onwards, the south and east coasts of Britain were harried by Germanic tribes. A Menapian Gaul, Carausius, was given the task of clearing the Channel of pirates. He did just this and then seized Britannia for his own. The breakaway state lasted from 287 to 296, but during this time it is probable that Carausius built forts along the east coast to repel the infiltrators. In the fourth century these were increased in number and an official responsible for both sides of the Channel (the 'count of the Saxon Shore') was created. Similar fort defences were built along the west coasts too, against the Irish.

But the barbarians were already within the gates. In the time of the emperor Marcus Aurelius (161–80), Germanic tribes had been officially settled in Britain. In the fourth century the Saxon Shore forts probably included men of Germanic origin in their forces. Units called *numeri,* composed of recruits from newly conquered areas, were brought into Britannia – in the third century these seem to have come almost entirely from Germanic lands. Britain was thus no stranger to Germanic tribesmen and there were undoubtedly many unofficial settlements too. These, like Topsy, just growed and growed. Existing enclaves were swelled as increasing numbers of tribesmen managed to avoid the already over-stretched defences of the Empire. There was probably also some social and cultural intermixture with the Romano-British, since it is possible to trace a distinctive Romano-Germanic culture in late Roman Britain. This is most evident from the pottery, which is an amalgam of the two styles. The culture was short-lived, however, since the Germanic population rapidly became dominant in the Dark Ages (p. 123). Roman Britain was already beginning to turn into Saxon England.

To the west and north of Britannia there were other barbarians. Like the Romano-British these were Celts, but their vigorous spirit had not been subdued by Classical culture. Only a turbulent strip of water separated the British from the Irish who, though more Romanized than might be imagined, nevertheless preserved a dynamic Celtic culture in many ways little different from that of pre-Roman Britain. During the Roman Iron Age the Irish Celts had their own troubles. The conflicts are reflected in later Irish saga. They could have been due to a population explosion prompted by increased food production. The outcome was displaced Irish Celts who chose first to raid and then to settle in western Britain. The famous folk hero Niall of the Nine Hostages was almost certainly a real person who harried the Western Isles of Scotland, possibly in 405. How early in history the raids gave way to settlement is difficult to assess, but it is clear that the Irish were a threat in Wales by the late third century and a positive menace by the fourth. To deal with the problem the Romano-British built new forts at Caernarvon and Holyhead in Anglesey, as well as at Lancaster and Cardiff. This may have delayed extensive colonization, but it did not prevent it. By the fifth century Argyll and the adjacent areas of western Scotland had been settled by the Scots from northern Ireland. The Irish settled in the Lleyn Peninsula, Pembroke, and the south Welsh coastal area. The Isle of Man suffered Irish incursions and Cornwall was colonized partly from Ireland and from the Irish in south Wales.

There were other Celtic trouble-makers too. At the end of the fourth century Britain north of the Forth–Clyde line was inhabited by various tribes who were still hostile to the Romans. The Caledonians who had fought Agricola had joined with other groups to form the Picts. The name is Roman and means the 'painted men', presumably because of tattoos. They called themselves Cruithni. The land of the Picts bordered the territory colonized by the Scots from Ireland.

The northern tribe most favourably disposed to the Romans was the Votadini. They had a long tradition of good relations with the Empire, and had been allowed to live in their hillfort of Traprain without disturbance. The British tribes of southern Scotland were thus in a vulnerable position, sandwiched between hostile Picts and Scots and the official frontier of Hadrian's Wall. The Roman attitude was simply to foster civilized ways amongst them and use them as buffers.

After various spasmodic troubles over the centuries, serious unrest came to the northern Roman frontier in 367 when a Celtic alliance of Picts, Scots and Attacotti (the identity of the latter is obscure) overran Hadrian's Wall. To deal with this 'Barbarian Conspiracy' one of the greatest military minds of the day, Theodosius, was sent to Britannia where he reorganized the defences. Hadrian's Wall and

109

some northern forts were restored to working order, signal stations were built along the Yorkshire coast and some town walls had bastions added.

Strife near the heart of the Empire necessitated the withdrawal of troops from Britannia over the following decades, and the province that had been so hard-won from the Celtic tribes was left vulnerable to barbarian attack from Celts and Saxons alike. The process was accelerated by a revolt under Magnus Maximus, who was proclaimed

56 Bronze coin struck by 'Carausius II'. The style of the coin is barbarous, indicative of an unofficial issue, and Carausius is not known from history – he must have been one of many usurpers in the fourth and fifth centuries. The coin was found at Richborough, Kent, and the reverse type is modelled on an official issue of 354–8

emperor by the army in Britannia in 383. He determined to make a bid for the purple in Rome and, taking with him considerable portions of the forces, eventually became master of Britain, Gaul, Spain and Africa. The success was short-lived and Maximus was finally defeated and executed on 28 July 388. The troops he had taken with him never returned and his revolt was thus of great significance in the British slide from civilization.

In 399 Stilicho the Vandal, general of the young emperor Honorius, turned his attention to restoring Britain after the barbarian raids. He was forced to abandon his efforts for Britannia, however, in 401 when the vicious Alaric attacked Italy with his Visigoths. Further troops were removed from Britain, including as Claudian wrote in a poem about AD 400, 'the legion deployed in far-off Britannia that curbs the savage Irish and reads the marks tattooed upon the bodies of dying Picts' (*De Bello Gothico,* 416–18). It was at about this time that Hadrian's Wall was abandoned by the military for ever. Gaul was overrun by barbarians and three short-lived emperors were set up by the Romano-British. Stilicho was executed for his failure and Rome fell to the barbarians in 410. No one in the Empire had time to care what happened in Britannia. None cared less than the emperor Honorius, who, when told in his Ravenna retreat that Rome had perished, thought he was being informed of the death of his pet hen, Roma.

The Romano-British cared, however – they had no mind to lose their civilization. They had cause to regret their choice of Emperor in 407 when Constantine III, realizing that the defence of Gaul was of paramount importance to Britain, crossed the Channel, taking what must have been the very last of the troops, and hammered the barbarians. Unfortunately this left Britannia totally defenceless and in 410 the Romano-British wrote a desperate appeal to Honorius asking for men and money for the defence of the province. The reply was realistic: the cities were told to look to their own defence.

Honorius was in many ways merely reiterating what was already official policy. For decades the army had been run down and defence had consisted of whatever means was most feasible: the new forts built in the third and fourth centuries, the stout walling around towns, the signalling systems along the coasts and, more significantly, the re-use of Iron Age hillforts.

It had been the tribal centres of the hillforts that came in for most antagonism from the Romans in the early years of conquest. The policy had been to breach the ramparts sufficiently to deter their use as centres of resistance and to remove the inhabitants to nearby Roman towns that were specially founded. As the population became Romanized the significance of the hillforts as possible danger areas would have diminished. It is not difficult to believe that officialdom would not have frowned on the refurbishing of the old citadels, and indeed may have encouraged it. The forts gave a ready-made solution to the problems of defence. Almost every convenient hilltop in Britain was already surrounded by ramparts and ditches, only partly destroyed. Furthermore, hillforts had been expressly conceived to shelter animals as well as humans. With the minimum of effort, expense and money they could be refurbished to meet with an emergency. It is unlikely that the forts thus spruced up in the fourth century were occupied permanently. They were perhaps regarded more in the manner of air-raid or fall-out shelters.

Hillforts had, however, been closely connected with religious observance in the Iron Age – some may even have originated as cult centres. Once the Romano-Britons were made conscious of the old places, memories of their ancestry seem to have come flooding back. On wind-swept hills, shrines sprang up, the cult centres of Celtic deities whose services had been dispensed with as the gods of Rome were seen to excel in the first century. Now the Empire was demonstrably not omnipotent against the barbarians, the Classical pantheon seemed to go out of favour too. Despite the popularity of Christianity in the late Roman period, more traditional deities were sought.

Within the ramparts of Maiden Castle where, nearly 400 years before, the Durotriges had tried to hold out against Vespasian's legion, a temple was built. It obviously prospered, for gold coins were discovered in its ruins. So too at Lydney, Gloucestershire, where a Celtic god, Nodens, became the focus for a centre of healing. It has been suggested that this deity was of Irish origin and reflected the local population's respect for the barbarians who were disrupting their shores. The shrine was built within the

57 (*Left*) Cadbury-Congresbury, Somerset, during excavation. This was an Iron Age hillfort, extensively refortified in the fifth century, when a ditch was dug into the rock to provide material for a flat-topped platform surmounted by a timber or turf façade. Occupation continued into the sixth century, and imported Mediterranean pottery appeared on the site quite late in the fifth century. The structure excavated is a circular timber building, about 11 m in diameter, broken by an entrance about 6 m wide. Its date is not certain, but it is more probably post- than pre-Roman

58 (*Right*) Liddington Castle, Berkshire, an Iron Age hillfort not far from Swindon. It has been claimed as the site of the battle of Mons Badonicus, where Arthur defeated the Anglo-Saxons. Excavation in 1976 showed refurbishing of the rampart in the late Roman or post-Roman period. The picture shows a section across the rampart in the south-west corner of the fort, looking west

defences of an old Iron Age hillfort, but grew to be a minor 'Lourdes' with guest accommodation for the sick.

Once begun, whether for defence or for religious purposes or both, the process of refortification accelerated during the last years of the fourth century and the early fifth. In some cases the ramparts were heightened and the ditches cleaned, but in others new ramparts, gates, even entirely new forts were constructed. The models for the new defences were not based on any ill-founded Celtic sentimentality for the past – they were Roman. South Cadbury, Somerset, refortified during this period, was given a gateway like that of a Roman fort.

The refurbishing of older defences cannot therefore be seen as a 'Celtic Revival'. The Celts had demonstrated their lack of 'national' pride in the early years of conquest, and did so once more in the Dark Ages. True Celtic pride is a much more recent phenomenon.

Hillforts were not the only method of defence that survived into the Dark Ages. Some Roman forts, too, were refurbished after the regular troops had been removed. Local leaders no doubt found the obsolete foundations the natural location for their new headquarters. In north Wales for instance, the old Roman buildings at Pen Llystyn were not in sufficient repair to warrant use. Instead the local leader set up a new palisade and timber buildings within it. In York, the Roman headquarters building continued to be used after the legion had left. Although the fate of the headquarters building is not known at Chester, the fortress survived the withdrawal of its military forces.

The withdrawal of Roman forces was thus of less dramatic effect than their arrival had been in 43. Life five or ten years before or after 410 was probably very similar for the average man. If the times were uncertain and standards of living were falling, it was merely part of a trend that had started well within the Roman period. Nevertheless, Britain was

effectively outside the Empire when Honorius refused them help. The inhabitants might call themselves Roman still, but without the strength of the legions this was little more than wishful thinking – what had been Britannia for nearly four centuries was now Celtic again.

It was therefore not by accident that many of the Celtic kingdoms that grew up in the fifth and sixth centuries were founded on the remnants of Roman administration. The Romano-British made the transition back to being Celts almost as easily, if not as willingly, as their ancestors had taken up with the Empire.

59 (*Left*) Dinas Emrys, Gwynedd, an Iron Age fort in Snowdonia re-occupied in the post-Roman period. Excavations in the 1950s showed it to have features in common with Scottish nuclear forts (i.e. its use of natural outcrop linked with sections of rampart), and revealed a 'pool' with associated structures. In legend it was here that Vortigern tried to build a tower but was told he could not do it until the blood of a fatherless child was sprinkled on the site – Ambrosius was nearly sacrificed to this end

60 (*Right*) Chun Castle, Cornwall. An Iron Age stone-walled fort re-occupied in the post-Roman period

Roman influence in the highland areas

While Celtic culture was being diluted to near extinction in the Civil Zone, life went on with remarkably little change in the highland areas and beyond the Imperial frontier. Uprisings were from time to time put down, but politics seem to have made very little impact on everyday life in parts of Wales, Cornwall or northern England, and virtually none at all in Scotland.

In these areas, unlike the more civilized south, there is even some evidence that hillforts were not all abandoned as the legions had advanced. In Wales, the impressive stone-built fort of Tre'er Ceiri in Gwynedd was still inhabited, as finds of Roman material, including a gold-plated bronze brooch, demonstrate. Indeed, it does not appear to have

113

been left nearly until the garrisons themselves left Wales.

In Scotland, too, lack of excavation on hillfort sites makes it difficult to assess whether their survival in the Roman period was rare or commonplace. The evidence tends to point to reduced occupation making like use of the original defences. Castle Law, Midlothian, has a souterrain that produced Roman finds of the second century AD dug into the innermost fort ditch, while other hillforts such as Burnswark, Dumfries and Woden Law, Roxburgh, were slighted and then used for Roman siege practice.

One fort in Scotland not only continued in occupation but actually grew in prosperity with Roman contact. This was Traprain Law, the seat of the pro-Roman Votadini of East Lothian. Here Roman finds were abundant, particularly those dating to the second century. Roman pottery was widely used by the inhabitants. Their own products, coarsely-gritted and very inferior to those of the Belgae, sometimes imitated Roman forms which, ironically, often owed something to Belgic design. Particularly interesting among the Romano-British objects at Traprain are distinctive dress fasteners some of which were apparently being imitated by local bronze-smiths. Towards the end of the second and during the first part of the third century, Traprain may have been abandoned, but Roman trade began again in the mid-third century and continued until the Dark Ages.

By the end of the fourth century the military occupation of Scotland was ended, though it is clear that diplomatic relations were maintained with client kingdoms. The fourth-century inhabitants of Traprain Law used Roman coins as money, possibly using them rather than barter, to buy Roman glassware and pottery. They were also literate,

61 A stone inscribed with the first letters of the alphabet, from the native fort at Traprain Law, East Lothian. This and another find from Traprain Law attest the presence there of literate Celts during the Roman period

and inscriptions found on pieces of pottery and stone include part of the alphabet and the latter half of a Roman name: (An)TONINUS. Literacy may have been necessary for keeping accounts. In the west, the Roman finds from Dalry, Ayrshire, might reflect a similar situation, with a client kingdom maintaining good relations with the Roman world. Apart from such obvious contacts with the Roman world, there was no break between Iron and Dark Ages in these areas.

One development of the native economy during the Roman period was the use of stone instead of wood for building. When stone was preferred in areas where timber was available it is almost as certain evidence for receptivity to civilized thought as were the Belgic coins.

There are several types of stone-built hut. They are a particular feature of north-west Wales where they became popular in the third century. Some, such as Cefn Graeanog, Hafoty-Wern-Las and Din Lligwy also contained rectangular or sub-rectangular buildings and are enclosed in polygonal yards. Rectilinear planning may betray Roman influence and it is possible that the hut groups represent the deliberate resettlement of native farmers in underpopulated areas. They were not, however, mere peasant farmsteads. Din Lligwy in Anglesey is palatial by northern standards, a sort of Celtic Fishbourne, set among a complex of fields.

In the Tyne–Forth region stone hut groups (enclosed by a stone wall) and open villages, made their appearance from the second century onwards, at the time when the local hillforts were falling out of use. As the forts became obsolete, huts were built in the ruins, or were put up on new sites, often in altitudes of over 300 m. In the Cheviots, the

62 Din Lligwy, Anglesey. A very large 'enclosed hut group' of a type found widespread in north Wales. A courtyard wall enclosed various structures, and here, as on some other sites, there was evidence of rectilinear planning, perhaps due to Roman influence. Din Lligwy has been described as a native version of the Roman palace at Fishbourne

115

settlements normally consist of round huts in a round or oval enclosure; in Northumberland there are signs of rectilinear planning. They were apparently enlarged or altered at various stages, and since they are notably impoverished it can be assumed that they had little or no contact with the military. Once established, however, the native hut groups persisted well into the Dark Ages. Huckhoe, Northumberland, and Crock Cleugh, Roxburgh, may have been occupied into the fifth century. St Cuthbert's Cell, to judge from description, may have been another thus long-lived. In Wales, Caer Mynydd, Gwynedd, and Pant-y-Saer, Anglesey, at least survived into the fifth century. Thus we have the interesting phenomenon of Celtic sites fostered by Roman officialdom in all probability and lasting into the Dark Ages.

In the south-west peninsula the tradition of building round stone huts was already established in the Iron Age, due, presumably, to a scarcity of timber. The settlements still flourished into the Roman period, in Cornwall – finds from the classic villages of Carn Euny and Chysauster show that there were still Celts living their traditional lives in the second century (p. 59). Porthmeor, in the Land's End peninsula, is a similar village, occupied in the late fourth and fifth century. The Dark Age settlement of Gwithian had stone huts that represent a survival of the Iron Age tradition and the same can be said of the recently excavated Trethurgy, occupied from the Roman period into the fifth or sixth centuries.

In general, however, the arrival of the Roman army had little effect on native lifestyles in border areas and beyond. In lowland Scotland, finds from sites such as Milton Loch, Kirkcudbright, and Lochlees, Ayrshire, show that crannogs (lake dwellings) were enjoying a new lease of life. North of the Antonine Wall life changed little if at all, though Roman merchandise travelled far and wide, reaching brochs such as Midhowe, Orkney, and Clickhimin, Shetland, in the second century. The factors which led to a decline in brochs and their replacement by round houses (p. 66) cannot be directly related to Roman influence, though the presence of an alien force in the south might have led to greater tribal unity in Atlantic Scotland.

Throughout the Roman occupation of the south, northern Celts took to trading with the soldier with enthusiasm. Roman objects that passed into Celtic hands include some of the finest finds from northern Britain – they were certainly not the rubbish looted from abandoned forts. Many of the northern Roman forts had annexes which, by the second century, accommodated such diverse peoples as Celtic ladies of easy virtue and traders such as the Salames who sold his wares at Bar Hill on the Antonine Wall. The annexes were probably flourishing markets. The trade currency seems to have been Roman coins: the coinage pattern found in forts is directly reflected in that of the second-century native sites. Roman merchandise included bronze vessels, brooches and glassware. In return the army acquired Celtic swords, wheels (if not chariots), horsegear, at least one torc, glass armlets, and even oysters which probably came from the Firth of Forth. Everyday Celtic objects such as deer-horn tools, weaving combs and spindles, beehive querns, stone lamps, stone discs and wooden dishes are not likely to have been traded for military use, but for the many hangers-on, unofficial families and entrepreneurs in the extra-mural settlements.

The 'drift' of Roman merchandise did not end with the abandonment of the Antonine Wall in the late second century. Although the flow of Roman objects to Scotland diminished, Celtic enterprise brought back some fine items to enrich northern homes. One example is a silver gilded crossbow brooch from the Moray Firth. Some of these goods were undoubtedly acquired through honest trade. Other items reached sticky Celtic fingers through looting, the finest example being the fourth-century hoard of silverwork

63 Some silver objects from the Traprain Treasure, found on the site of this East Lothian hillfort in 1919. The treasure had been hammered down ready for melting, and probably represents loot carried north by Celtic raiders from some southern villa or town, perhaps even from as far afield as Gaul. Late fourth century

from Traprain Law, partly hammered down by pirates in readiness for the melting pot. The story told by the finds and by the buildings in the border areas and beyond is that borne out by inferences from the Dark Ages – by the time the Romans left Britannia even the most hostile areas were not averse to Roman possessions. Like the tribes in the south who had been 'softened up' after Caesar's conquest until they were receptive to Classical thought, those in the north had begun to modify their views. Before civilization had taken hold, however, the Roman legions had left and Celtic culture triumphed once more.

The Dark Ages   Chapter four

The Pillar of Eliseg is a stone cross-shaft which stands on a wind-swept hillock in the Vale of Llangollen, looking towards the medieval abbey of Valle Crucis. Nothing can be seen on it now, except an inscription commemorating its

64   The Pillar of Eliseg, Llangollen, Denbighshire. It carries a long inscription (now only partly legible) which relates how it was set up by king Concenn of Powys (who is known to have died in 854) to commemorate his great-grandfather. The type of the cross, however, is Mercian English and of the tenth–eleventh centuries, and its inscription poses many problems

re-erection in the eighteenth century. Perhaps the eye of faith can make out a few faint letters, long since weathered from the stone, but they were not always indiscernible. In 1696 Edward Lhwyd, the indefatigable Welsh antiquary, visited the stone on his travels round Wales and transcribed its inscription, which ran to 31 lines (traces of 15 have been noticed this century) (translated by V. E. Nash-Williams, *Early Christian Monuments of Wales*, Cardiff, 1950):

> Concenn son of Cattell, Cattell son of Brohcmail, Brohcmail son of Eliseg, Eliseg son of Guoillauc. Concenn, who is therefore great-grandson of Eliseg, erected this stone to his great-grandfather Eliseg. Eliseg annexed the inheritance of Powys . . . throughout nine [years] from the power of the English, which he made into a sword-land by fire. . . . Britu moreover [was] the son of Guorthigirn [Vortigern] whom Germanus blessed and whom Severa bore to him, the daughter of Maximus, the king, who killed the king of the Romans. . . .

This inscription implies that the stone was set up by a king Concenn of Powys, who history tells us died in 854, to commemorate his great-grandfather, whose genealogy is given. Already the mystery has begun. Why should Concenn want to commemorate his great-grandfather? His father yes, even perhaps his grandfather. But in the Dark Ages men were seldom interested in praising their remote forebears, unless for a political end, and where politics are at stake, the bending of history must be suspected. Second, there is good reason to suppose the cross-shaft was not set up in the time of Concenn. The type of cross is Mercian, of the late tenth or even eleventh century. But Concenn must have set it up sometime in the first half of the ninth century, if the text is to be believed. Yet at this date Mercian influence in sculpture would be surprising in Wales; at an eleventh-century date it would be incredible. Furthermore, the English are described as Angli, but in ninth-century Wales they would have been called Saxons. Was the pillar an eleventh-century hoax, set up for some political end? If so, how much of the information it contains is genuine, compiled from real sources, and how much a figment of eleventh-century imagination?

The latter part of the inscription gives information about two key personalities in the story of Dark Age Britain – Magnus Maximus (p. 110) and Vortigern the 'proud tyrant' who by inviting Hengist and Horsa to Britain as fifth-century mercenaries traditionally started the Dark Ages. If the secret of this and other similarly enigmatic inscriptions could be unlocked, some of the problems of the Dark Ages might be solved.

The Pillar of Eliseg illuminates the difficulties besetting scholars of the Dark Ages. Until recently this century Dark Age studies consisted of antiquaries grappling with such insoluble problems. Archaeology was not advanced enough to be used as an approach to the period. The written word was sparse, often untrue and usually distorted. Historians did their best and passed on to more fruitful subjects. Besides, who much before the twentieth century really wanted to know about the barbarians? Historians' own training put them in sympathy with the earlier chroniclers who had copied Dark Age sources with unconcealed bias.

The three chief sources for written Dark Age history are the Celts Gildas and Nennius and the Anglo-Saxon Bede. It is remarkable that anything survives at all, yet the sources are tantalizingly confusing.

The blame for a great deal of the confusion surrounding the fifth- and early sixth-century British history must lie with Gildas, a western British monk of literary genius but strong historical prejudice. He died around 572 and wrote a rhetorical polemic known as the *De Excidio Britanniae*, 'Concerning the ruin and conquest of Britain'. This contains statements now known not to be true – for instance he attributes the second-century walls of Hadrian and Antoninus Pius to the end of the fourth century. The information about Gildas' own time could be supposed to be historically less distorted, except that Gildas was not trying to write history. Here is Gildas at his most typical, in Camden's translation in *Britannia* (1695), describing the post-Roman period whose ills he describes and interprets entirely in moral Christian terms:

the wickedness of our Britain was without end. The enemies left us, but we would not leave our vices. For it has ever been the custom of this nation (as it is now at this day) to be feeble in repelling an enemy but valliant in civil wars, and in carrying on a course of sin, etc. . . . for during the forebearance of former ravages, the kingdom enjoyed such extensive plenty as was never remember'd in any age before: which is ever accompanied by debauchery. For it then grew to so high a pitch it might be truly said at the time 'Here is such fornication as was never among the Gentiles'. Nor was this the only prevailing sin of that age, but all other vices that can be imagined incident to human nature especially (which also now this day overthrow all goodness among us) a spight to truth and the teachers of it, a fondness for lyes and those that forge them, imbracing evil for good and a veneration for lewdness instead of virtue, a desire for darkness rather than light, and entertaining Satan before an Angel of light.

Powerful stuff, but what does it tell us of history?

Fortunately, there are a few other sources which provide corroboration, elaboration, and in some cases negation of Gildas' account. The most important of these is a compilation ascribed to a ninth-century Celtic monk, Nennius, which is in reality a collection of separate sources set down for the first time in the tenth century under the blanket name of the *Historia Britonnum*, the 'History of the Britons'. This was simply a collection and transcription of available documents. Disarmingly 'he' wrote of it: 'I have made a heap of all that I have found, from the annals of the Romans, the writings of the saints, the annals of the Irish and the Saxons and the traditions of our own old men.' Most of this 'heap' is nonsense by modern terms, but some sections can be used with confidence since they were set down at the time of the events they were recording, and refer to real happenings and personages. The *Historia Britonnum* is a primary source for any study of the early Celtic Dark Ages.

The third major source is concerned more with Anglo-Saxon affairs than with Celtic. This is the Venerable Bede's *Historia Ecclesiae*, 'Ecclesiastical History of the English Nation', which effectively begins with the arrival of St Augustine in 597. As its name suggests, it is more concerned with the affairs of the Church than the deeds of Men. Bede, whose account appeared in 731, was a Northumbrian monk, and the main concern of his writing was Northumbria, for which he is an invaluable and indisputable source. Before 597 Bede's account is based on a variety of sources, of which the most obvious is Gildas. Bede tried his best to make sense of the material at his disposal, drawing upon Continental sources where these seemed to help, but his rationalization of early British history holds nothing new for us, and we are forced back to Gildas and the *Historia Britonnum*.

These, then, are the main written sources for the earlier part of the Dark Ages in Britain. They are supplemented by a bewildering variety of subsidiary sources – Continental references to events in Britain, letters, saints' lives, poems, annals, law codes.

Modern archaeology has given some further information about the period but has brought its own problems. First archaeological method is still not far enough advanced to retrieve the information we might guess to be possible. Second, once retrieved the information is difficult to interpret, and third, as the period progressed the links with datable material from the Roman period and Continental imports became progressively less. Society became conservative, and material goods stayed similar for centuries. The tendency of the Dark Age Celts to use objects in wood, leather, cloth and basketry that under Rome would have been manufactured in more durable material has left few material remains.

The ghost of Britannia
In the areas which had been within the Roman jurisdiction, the Dark Age development was markedly different from that outside the Imperial boundaries. The area was already

more open to Continental influence, had already played host to Germanic tribes, and was familiar with Germanic peoples from those drafted into the Roman army. It was this area too that was the first land to which the Germanic Angles, Saxons, Jutes, Franks and others came when they crossed the Channel in the fifth and early sixth century from their Continental homelands. It was these who gave their name to England and who emerged as dominant in the Dark Ages.

The new tribes do not always seem to have been hostile, and it is notable that Romano-British life continued in many ways unmolested well into the fifth century. The early Germanic settlements that are known do not seem to have been defended at all, suggesting that the population was not generally hostile to them.

Why then did the Dark Ages happen? How could people with all the advantages of a highly developed civilization descend into the relatively illiterate, pagan squalor we have to accept was the case by and large in the seventh century? Although it can be argued that the Saxon courts of the seventh century were not totally primitive they were in no way comparable to the splendours of, for instance, Fishbourne in the first century AD.

There were undoubtedly many reasons, but a few might usefully be emphasized. First, the Roman way of life depended entirely on a strong central government and this, in 410, was dramatically removed with no real provision for the future. Opportunities for personal advancement of local leaders were abundant. It was thus only a short step to civil war. This was accelerated by the appearance of increasing numbers of Germanic tribesmen who were certainly involved in the disputes of the fifth and sixth centuries – whether against their kinsfolk (witness the dykes in East Anglia, built to defend Angles from Angles), or the Romano-British. Significantly too the Anglo-Saxons were geared to life without a central administration. As such they were a vigorous, innovating force in the population. Finally the Romano-British Celts seem to have paid dearly for their adherence to Roman life. In the sixth century a great plague ravaged Europe. This Yellow Peril was the bubonic plague, and its spread across Europe can be traced in contemporary accounts. It started in Egypt around 541 or 542, reaching Constantinople in 543, then spreading out across Europe as a whole. In 544 it reached the middle Rhine and also Ireland. Before this particularly virulent outbreak there had certainly been others. The plague attacked just those communities that were attempting to maintain a Roman lifestyle by keeping close trading and personal contacts with civilization. The walls that defended Romano-British towns from external attack must have contributed to the spread of the plague. Even as the British and Saxons were beginning to have some contacts, society was disrupted.

The Roman ways prevailed into the fifth century, however, despite these tragedies. Local administrations were built up on the bases of late Roman organization. Paradoxically it was those areas where Romanization was least

65 Wansdyke, a linear earthwork in two sections, not necessarily contemporary. This section of East Wansdyke, looking east between Easton Down and Tan Hill, may have been erected by the Britons against the early Saxon settlers in the Thames valley. The name means Wodens Dyke, i.e. it is named after a pagan Saxon god, suggesting it was in existence before the conversion of Wessex in the 630s

well established that have provided the greatest evidence for a continuation of Roman institutions, for it was these areas that were least affected by the Anglo-Saxon settlements. Scotland, Wales and Cornwall provide most information, Cornish memorial stones of the fifth and sixth centuries carry Roman names, and the king in this area in the time of Gildas still had a name with good Roman antecedents – Constantine. Gildas mentions another king in the south-west, Aurelius Caninius, who may have been based on Gloucester, suggesting that such kingdoms took root in other parts of Britain before they were swept away by the Anglo-Saxon advance.

The legacy of Rome was felt too in the survival of Latin. There is little doubt that the Celtic leaders of Britain in the fifth and sixth century had a knowledge of the language, and Latin loan-words aided the development of the Celtic languages in the fifth and sixth centuries. The Latin of Vortigern and king Arthur was that of the educated classes of Roman Britain. It was an upper-class Latin, insular, but not spoken with the same disregard for grammar that afflicted the speakers of Vulgar Latin in most of the provinces of the later Roman Empire. How long it survived is difficult to guess, but Celtic seems to have replaced it in courtly circles in the seventh century – the last bold clarion call of Latin culture appears on the tombstone of king Cadfan in Anglesey (p. 134) who died about 625. His successors were Celtic speakers, even if their language was coloured with words taken from a Roman past.

The somewhat artificial purity of British Latin meant that British schools were in favour for the sons of rich Gauls, and these academies survived into the fifth century and probably beyond. Richborough seems to have had contacts with the Continent at the end of the Roman period, and the Continental poet Ausonius refers to it. A certain Riocatus, who may have been the son of Vortigern, is recorded about 478 as taking back to Britain books written in Gaul. The standard of British scholarship was kept up to scratch in the fifth century by the comings and goings between Britain and the Continent. Letters were passed back and forth across the Channel, and learned men from both sides travelled widely in each other's lands. A lady commemorated on a tombstone at Llantrisant in Anglesey was married to a Gaul called Bivatigirnus, probably from Angers, and an influx of exiles from Roman Gaul into Ireland in the Dark Ages brought new standards of Classical learning there. In both Britain and Ireland wise men still survived who, amazingly, kept alive the traditions of the druids, and it so happened that the type of highly artificial rhetoric admired by the Celts was also the type of literature favoured in decadent Classical circles. St Patrick, in his writings, imitated St Augustine of Hippo, whose works must have been readily available in fifth-century Britain, while Gildas a century later followed a literary tradition which was firmly in the mainstream of Classical culture.

Individually, these clues amount to little, but taken along with the evidence of continuing life in many Romano-British towns through the fifth and into the sixth century it amounts to a strong body of evidence. When St Cuthbert visited Carlisle in the seventh century he walked round the walls and was shown a fountain built there by the Romans, implying some continuity of the town and also some measure of civic pride. In spite of the many factors working against their aspirations, St Albans and Silchester survived as towns until the end of the sixth century, and, in the frontier areas, Exeter, Wroxeter and less certainly York and Caerwent outlived the troubles of the greater part of the fifth century if not the sixth.

Nevertheless, the Romano-Britons had little chance against the multitude of misfortunes that beset them, and we can have some sympathy with Gildas when he categorically attributed the problems of the time to a simple matter of sin and its retribution. Thus does he sum up the end of Roman Britain, again in the seventeenth-century translation from the antiquary William Camden:

> The Romans having now withdrawn their forces, and abandoned Britain, the whole frame of affairs fell into disorder and misery; Barbarians invading it on one hand, and the inhabitants breaking out into factions on the other; whilst each one was for usurping the Government for himself. . . . But this woeful destruction of Britain shall be represented (or rather deplored) to you in the melancholy words of Gildas the *Britain*, all in tears at the thought of it. 'The Romans being drawn home, there descend in great crowds, from the little narrow bores of their Carroghes or Carts, wherein they were brought over the Scitick vale, about the middle of summer, in a scorching hot season, a dusking swarm of vermine, or hideous crew of Scots and Picts, somewhat different in manners but alike in thirsting after blood; who, finding that their old confederates [the Romans] were marched home, and refused to return any more, put on greater boldness than ever and possessed themselves of the North . . . to withstand this invasion, the towers [along the Wall] are defended by a lazy garrison, undisciplined, and too cowardly to ingage an enemy; being enfeebled with continual sloth and *idleness*. In the mean while the naked enemy advance with their hooked weapons by which the miserable *Britains*, pulled down from the tops of the walls, are dashed against the ground. To those that were destroyed after this manner, had this advantage in an untimely death, that they escaped these miserable sufferings which immediately befell their brothers and children.

Given a more modern bias, the story would be that the Saxons increased at the expense of the already waning Romano-British population until by the seventh century they had formed discernible and important kingdoms. Of the personalities who people this period, Vortigern and Arthur are popularly the best known.

Vortigern came into prominence around 425. His name is an epithet meaning 'Overking' – Gildas translated it as 'Proud Tyrant'. He was a man in the same mould as Maximus and Constantine III, a notable of Gloucester who assumed control and invited the Jutes Hengist and Horsa to settle in Kent as part of a wider policy of settling federates. Gildas tells the story in his own inimitable prose:

> The brood of cubs burst from their lair of the barbarian lioness, in three Keels as they call warships in their tongue. . . . At the orders of the accursed tyrant, they fixed their fearful claws upon the eastern part of the island, as though to defend it. . . . Their dam, learning the success of the first contingent, sent over a

larger draft of the satellite dogs. . . . Thus were the barbarians
introduced . . . in the guise of soldiers taking great risks for their
generous 'hosts' as the liars asserted. They demanded supplies
which were granted, and for a long time shut the dog's mouth.

Vortigern's objective was to muster forces with which to
push back Pictish and Irish raiders in the north. Either the
presence or the threat of increased forces was effective: the
northern raids were curbed. But the path now lay open for
the Germanic incomers. Archaeology has proved that already
in the time of Vortigern there were considerable settlements
and by the time of his death around 461, much of south-east
England was probably under Germanic control. From then
on the tide of affairs ebbed and flowed, with sometimes the
British, sometimes the Anglo-Saxons more successful.

At the time of Vortigern's death another champion of
Roman Britain emerged: Ambrosius Aurelianus, a resis-
tance leader whose father may have been an enemy of
Vortigern. Gildas describes him as 'perhaps the last of the
Romans to survive, whose parents had worn the purple
before they were killed in the fury of the storm'. Almost
nothing else is known about him. He probably commanded
British resistance until the 470s, and was succeeded by
Arthur.

Arthur – Celt, Roman, and king

The story of king Arthur's Christian battles against the
Saxons is one of the most magical in the English language,
but modern research has shown that the legends are based
in fact. Arthur was in fact a British leader in the mould of
many before him, except that he was almost certainly very
Romanized in outlook and was fighting not only for Christianity but for civilization.

The authenticity of Arthur as a historical figure lies in the
final analysis of two sentences, probably first set down at the
time of the events they describe and later incorporated into a
table for calculating the date of Easter. In the entry for the
year 518 the annal reads: 'The battle of Badon in which
Arthur carried the Cross of our Lord Jesus Christ on his
shoulders for three days and nights and the Britons were
victorious.' The second entry reads, for AD 539, 'The strife
of Camlann in which Arthur and Modred perished, and
there was plague in Britain and Ireland.'

This Easter Table is a fairly reliable addition to Nennius'
compilation. Another reference in Nennius is less reliable:
based on an epic poem about Arthur, it gives an account
of the twelve battles fought by him, the last listed being
that of Mons Badonicus, Mount Badon. This text is certainly

127

older than the ninth century and is based on a Welsh original which could have been set down soon after Arthur's death.

Arthur, then, can confidently be described as a Christian leader of the Britons, who fought against their enemies, presumably the Saxons, and was killed along with someone called Modred, at the battle of Camlann, arguably *c.* 539. Before that he had fought several other battles, and had won a resounding victory, perhaps at Mount Badon.

66 Page from the British Museum Harley MS 3859, folio 190a. These Easter Annals added to a group of texts reputedly collected by a ninth-century Welsh monk, Nennius. This page has computations for Easter and annalistic notes to make them memorable. In the right-hand column the long entry is the reference to Arthur's battle at Mons Badonicus, and at the bottom of the column is an entry referring to his last battle, Camlann. On this text Arthur's historicity in great measure depends. The manuscript dates from the early twelfth century

Gildas does not mention Arthur by name (a fact which has led some historians to believe Arthur never existed), but he does report that the Anglo-Saxon advance was halted for a while by Ambrosius Aurelianus. He also reports that 'From that time on sometimes the British were victorious, sometimes the enemy, up to the year of the siege of Mons Badonicus, which was almost the most recent but not the least slaughter of the gallows crew.' This battle, affirms Gildas, was fought in the year of his birth, and in the subsequent forty-four years Britain had enjoyed freedom from external attack though not from civil strife. From this it can be assumed that some time around the beginning of the sixth century the battle of Mons Badonicus halted the Anglo-Saxon advance.

As will be seen, the legend of Arthur lived on in exaggerated form – the historical figure has been unravelled only in the past decade. But Celtic culture, with its strong Roman overlay, was finished in what became England. The Anglo-Saxons were, like the Romans before them, the more dynamic force, and Celtic development was at an end in their areas.

Arthur and his contemporaries managed to halt the Anglo-Saxon expansion in the west, until shortly after the middle of the sixth century. By this time Germanic settlement had extended to the Humber and North Lincolnshire, to East Anglia, Essex, Middlesex, Sussex, Hampshire and Kent, and their advance in the upper Thames was held back by. Arthur's victories.

The British recovery may have gained some lost ground, but soon after 550 the Saxons were pushing westwards again, defeating the British at Salisbury. Buckingham was overwhelmed, and in 577 western Britain was cut off following an overwhelming Saxon victory at the battle of Dyrham, when Bath, Cirencester and Gloucester were lost.

Some Britons seem to have maintained their identity in the marsh lands of the Somerset levels, but in 614 the Anglo-Saxons moved into Devon, and by 682 they were effectively in control. Cornwall, however, was left to its own devices for some time to come. Here there was a succession of local kings, such as Dungarth who is commemorated on the ninth-century King Doniert's Stone which still stands 4.8 km north-west of Liskeard. From the ninth century, however, Cornwall became progressively Anglicized. In 926 Aethelstan received the submission of Huwal, king of Cornwall, and the area was absorbed into the kingdom of England.

Meanwhile, Anglo-Saxon England had been crystallizing

129

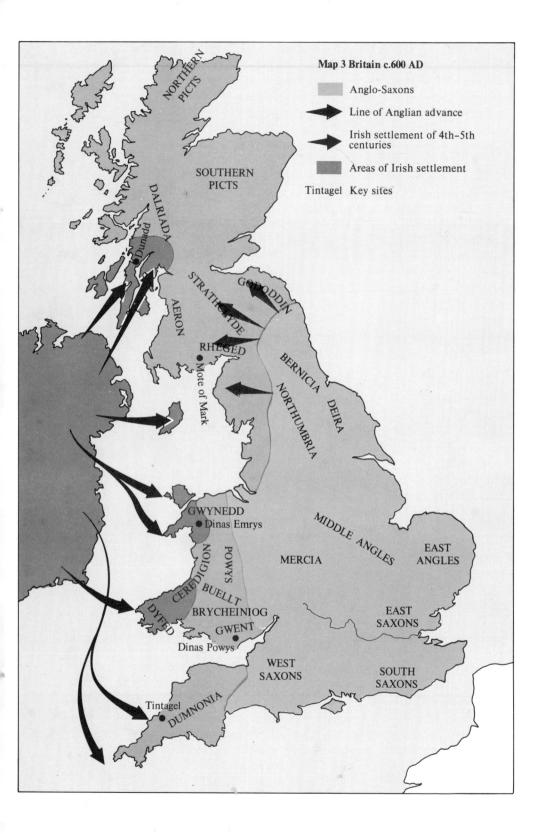

Map 3 Britain c.600 AD

Anglo-Saxons

Line of Anglian advance

Irish settlement of 4th–5th centuries

Areas of Irish settlement

Tintagel Key sites

NORTHERN PICTS

SOUTHERN PICTS

DALRIADA

Dunadd

AERON

STRATHCLYDE

GODODDIN

RHEGED

Mote of Mark

BERNICIA

DEIRA

NORTHUMBRIA

GWYNEDD

Dinas Emrys

MIDDLE ANGLES

EAST ANGLES

POWYS

CEREDIGION

BUELLT

DYFED

BRYCHEINIOG

GWENT

Dinas Powys

MERCIA

EAST SAXONS

WEST SAXONS

SOUTH SAXONS

Tintagel

DUMNONIA

itself into the Heptarchy. The first kingdoms to gain supremacy were those of Kent and East Anglia: by the mid-seventh century they were eclipsed by Northumbria. Broadly speaking, south of the Thames the people were predominantly Saxons. North of it, the Angles were in the majority. Northumbria emerged out of the fusion of two Anglian kingdoms, Bernicia and Deira, and in the time of Bede extended from Yorkshire to the Lothians. In the eighth century Northumbria was eclipsed by the central English kingdom of Mercia, which rose to prominence under its famous leader Offa. Just as the Northumbrians harried the Celts, so too did the Mercians, who pressed particularly on the Welsh on their western border. But Mercia in its turn was to be eclipsed, this time by Wessex, which first attained prominence under Alfred the Great. It was one of the West Saxon successors of Alfred, Aethelstan, who effectively united Anglo-Saxon England into a unified kingdom around 927.

Early Wales

By the time of Arthur, kingdoms had started to take shape in northern Britain and Wales. The process must have been effected easily since it was based on the remnants of Roman administration. The strength and endurance of Roman institutions can be traced well into the sixth century by the survival of names and titles and by the occupation of old Roman sites.

·Tombstones of the fifth and sixth centuries imply continuity of Roman thought and institutions. From Penmachno, not far from the Roman fort of Segontium (Caernarvon), comes a fifth-century stone with inscriptions that include the terms *civis* and *magistratus* (i.e. 'citizen' and 'magistrate'). Such terms are Roman in conception and would have been completely meaningless unless there was some survival of Roman provincial organization in north Wales in the fifth century.

The memorial stones of the fifth and sixth centuries provide other clues to the survival of an ordered, Roman-derived lifestyle in Wales. A stone from Llangian (Gwynedd) commemorates a *medicus* (doctor), while personal names of purely Roman origin are commonplace: Bona, Nobilis, Paulinus, Martius, Salvianus, Cupetianus, Secundus, Terpillius, Justus, Martinus, Carausius, Paterninus, Victorinus, Severus and many others.

Roman forts were still occupied into the Dark Ages and their organization must have been the blueprint for the new administrations. Aberffraw fort in Angelsey became the seat of the princes of Gwynedd and Caernarvon fortress was furnished with a new guard chamber for one of its gates. Wales had been one of the areas that the late Roman administration had considered in need of help in its defensive policy. The method employed was of inviting barbarians from elsewhere to settle and repel the foe, this time the Irish. The most direct evidence for this lies in the story of Cunedda. This man was leader of the Votadini from Traprain Law, Scotland, and some time in the 380s, when

67 Fifth-century tombstone at Llangian, Gwynedd, commemorating Melus *medicus*, i.e. a doctor. This is evidence for the survival of some Romano-British standards in fifth-century Wales

the Roman army was greatly depleted in Britannia, he was invited to settle in north Wales. He and his followers were responsible for the eventual founding of a new kingdom in Wales. A Welsh medieval folktale keeps alive a ghostly memory of the event: 'Maxen Wledig was emperor of Rome, and a comlier and a better and a wiser was he than any before him.' The story is that of the *Dream of Maxen Wledig*, and tells how Maxen dreams of a beautiful lady whom he eventually finds and marries. She is known as Helen Luyddawc, Helen of the Hosts. This folktale is notable for several reasons. Maxen Wledig is none other than the usurper Magnus Maximus. He is described as having done some wonderful but unspecified thing for Wales. Helen's castle is Caernarvon and the two Roman sites of Caerleon and Carmarthen also figure prominently in the tale. Could it be that the wonderful thing Maximus did for Wales was to set up the administrative machinery that led to the formation of the early Welsh kingdoms?

It is likely that it was Maximus who sent the invitation to Cunedda to settle in Wales – the date is right and it fits the known facts. What is more significant is that Maximus figures in several Welsh genealogies as well as his mention on the Pillar of Eliseg (p. 120).

The kingdom traditionally founded by Cunedda became Gwynedd and extended to Anglesey. In the time of Gildas it was ruled over by Maelgwn, who is described by the historian as the 'dragon of the isles'. More is known about him than about many early kings. His youth was devoted to the church, but in the mid-sixth century he changed character and became a ruthless heroic chieftain remembered by medieval Welsh poets, celebrated by Taliesin and in the story of the *Dream of Rhonabwy*. His people are also sometimes known as the Venedotians, and his own seat was at Deganwy, a craggy rock which now looks out across holiday homes and towards Llandudno and the Ormes.

Maelgwn died of the 'yellow plague'. In later medieval romance, the plague became a hideous monster, the 'yellow spectre' which Maelgwn saw through a keyhole (translated by J. E. Lloyd, *Outlines of the History of Wales*, Caernarvon, 1906, p. 83):

The strange beast shall come
From the ladies marsh
With vengeance for sin
Upon Maelgwn Gwynedd
Its hair and its teeth
And its eyes shall be saffron
And it shall bring death
To Maelgwyn Gwynedd.

In Gildas' time, Dyfed (modern Pembroke) was ruled over by Vortepor, whose ancestry can be traced back to Magnus Maximus. His family tree is given in an early source as 'Maxen guletic map Protec map Protector' ('Maxen Wledig, son of Protec, son of Protector'). *Protector* (and its corruption Protec) is a title, not a personal name, and on Vortepor's tombstone, which was found at Castell Dwyran in south Wales, he is described as 'Vortepor Protector'. But the title is Roman, given to officer-cadets in the late Roman army. From this it can be inferred that Magnus Maximus set up in Dyfed an administration which was Roman-based and possibly supervised by a military official. One genealogy gives Vortepor's grandfather as Triphun, again a blundered title. What was meant was *tribunus*, the commander of a military unit.

The origins of the other Welsh kingdoms are less clear. Some stemmed from the tribal organization of Wales, others traced their dynasties to Roman times. *Gwerthrynion* takes its name from its legendary founder Vortigern – *Buelt* also had a line traced back to him.

Up to the seventh century Wales and Cumbria were closely linked: the Welsh spoke affectionately of their northern contemporaries as the 'Gwŷr y Gogledd', the Men of the North. There were, too, links with the small kingdom of Elmet in the south of the Yorkshire Pennines, though these were broken when the area was conquered by Edwin of Northumbria around 617. The severance of Wales and Cumbria was the work of the Anglo-Saxons and early Welsh history is in great part the story of the uneasy relationship between Celt and Saxon.

By the seventh century Gwynedd emerged as the dominant state in Wales, achieving prominence first under the leadership of Cadfan (Catamanus). His tombstone is still preserved at Llangadwaladr church in Anglesey and describes him as 'Catamanus, wisest and most renowned of all kings'. The proud boast has an exotic ring about it, and echoes the phraseology of the Byzantine court, hinting that forgotten splendours may have coloured court life in seventh-century Wales.

Cadfan's successor was Cadwallon, who campaigned against the Northumbrians under Edwin. Later Welsh traditions asserted that Edwin spent part of his youth in Anglesey. He was described as one of the 'Three Great Oppressions of Mona, nurtured within the Island'. Cadwallon's early campaigns against Edwin were not altogether successful, though bards described one of his battles as one of the Three Pollutions of the Severn, because, it was said, the blood of the warriors reddened the river 'from its source to its estuary'. Cadwallon subsequently allied with the mighty Penda of Mercia, and between them they defeated and killed Edwin at Hatfield Chase in 632. Cadwallon's successor, Cadafael the Wild, did little for Gwynedd, though his son, Cadwaladr, revived the old fighting spirit of the Celts.

Penda of Mercia, although an ally of convenience, was nevertheless bent on the expansion of his own territory on the frontiers of Wales. During his lifetime Mercia was extended along the upper Severn and into Cheshire, where a new buffer state was set up between Wales and Mercia known as *Magonsaetan*, centred on the Hereford plain and the south Shropshire highlands. This was ruled over by a Northumbrian family who had aided Penda in the war against Edwin.

Mercian aggression was felt mostly by the Welsh border kingdom of Powys. Nevertheless, peace was maintained into the early eighth century, when Welsh aggression and raiding brought the problems of the frontier into sharp focus. Following particularly severe raids in 705 and 709 the Mercians set about building a boundary. This was to take the form of the earthwork now known as Wat's Dyke, usually associated with Aethelbald (AD 716–57) but which need not greatly pre-date the more substantial earthwork built by Offa. As it survives today, Wat's Dyke averages about 1.2 m in height and 15.2 in width, and runs from Basingwerk (Flints) to the Morda between Oswestry and Maesbury in Shropshire. Its construction had the desired psychological effect on the Welsh, and encouraged some table-turning on the part of the Mercians, who grew bold in their new security and began to harry Powys. The culmination of their offensive was the construction of Offa's Dyke, the mighty rampart which is, along with Wat's Dyke, one of the most outstanding archaeological remains in Britain. In terms of length they put Hadrian's Wall to shade – it is a mere 117.5 km in length. Offa's Dyke is 193.1 km long and runs almost unbroken through some of the most breathtaking scenery in England, from Treuddyn to a point near Chepstow on the Severn, the gaps now apparent being closed at the time by dense forest. It was a frontier, not a military work, and no forts defend its length.

The subsequent history of Wales is simply traced. Much of it reads like historical romance, with marriage alliances reducing the number of kingdoms. At the end of the eighth century a remote descendant of Maelgwn, Merfyn Vrych, rose to prominence in Gwynedd. He was determined to open up the country to outside stimulus. His court was in contact with that of Charles the Bald at Liège, and this cosmopolitan outlook was continued by his son, Rhodri Mawr. Under Rhodri, Gwynedd became the dominant kingdom in Wales, and his court was the focus for a cultural renaissance which led to the setting down of much oral tradition, to the benefit of posterity. His career was not entirely peaceful. He kept the Vikings out of Wales and carried on a continuous struggle against Mercia and Wessex on the eastern front.

His campaigns ended in tragedy. He met his death at the

hands of the Saxons and Mercia succeeded in gaining extensive control in Wales. From then on Welsh history was a chronicle of English aggression. Within Wales, some supported union with England, while others, in the tradition of many Celts before them, were bitterly opposed to it. The matter was settled by Rhodri Mawr's grandson, Hywel Dda, who, having unified all Wales, launched a pro-English policy by making friendly overtures to Aethelstan, king of all England. By 931 Hywel was virtually a client king of

68 Free-standing cross, Carew, Pembroke. One of a series of late crosses in Wales, this is the finest of a small group in Pembrokeshire. The inscription on the front records that it is the 'cross of Margiteut, son of Etguin', who can be identified as Maredudd ap Edwin, the fifth in descent from Hywel Dda. The cross can thus be dated to between 1033 and 1035

Aethelstan, and when he died in 949 or 950 much of Wales was pro-Anglian. In the mountains of the north, however, anti-English feeling ran strong and flared up time and time again to the present day.

Early Scotland

As these events were unfolding in Wales, a comparable saga was shaping the history of Scotland. In the late fifth century four groups of peoples were fighting for supremacy north of Hadrian's Wall. Between the Wall and the Forth–Clyde line the population mainly comprised Britons – men like the Welsh who spoke an allied tongue, who were descended from the Iron Age Celts, and who had escaped Roman domination. To the north of the Antonine Wall lay Picts and Scots, the former the indigenous inhabitants of north-east Scotland. The latter were immigrants from Ireland who, having come first as raiders, had in the fifth century settled in the under-populated areas of western Scotland. A fourth group eventually pressed on natives and incomers alike: these were the Angles of Northumbria, who, by the seventh century, made themselves virtually masters of the Scottish Lowlands.

Britons

In the Lowlands various kingdoms had crystallized out of late Roman administrative origins. In the late fourth century Theodosius had probably established the office of *Dux Britanniorum*, Count of the Britons, whose administrative centre may have been at York. Responsible to him were the Popular Prefects, *Praefecti Gentium*, who were sent out to set up regional administrations among the pro-Roman tribes on the frontier. This is particularly apparent north of Hadrian's Wall, where the names of some of the prefects are known from later genealogies. They were the founders of the Dark Age Celtic kingdoms, and their names are fossilized under a thin Celtic disguise. In effect Roman officials were the first kings of Dark Age Britain.

How long there were 'Roman' officials in Dark Age Britain, and how soon they were replaced by men who regarded themselves as kings is uncertain. If we must seek a changeover, one man seems a likely candidate. He is Coel Hên, Old King Cole, a familiar figure from the nursery, who lived in the early fifth century and was perhaps the last Dux and the first High King of Dark Age Britain. No fewer than eight dynasties of early Scotland claimed descent from him, perhaps more truthfully from the *praefecti* he sent out rather than from Coel himself.

Among the Praefecti Gentium two were sent out in the late fourth century to supervise affairs in Votadini country. One, Catellius Decianus, oversaw the north. The other, Paternus, was responsible for the south. The *praefectus* Quintillius Clemens was sent to the region round Dumbarton that grew into the Dark Age kingdom of Alclud and subsequently Strathclyde. His grandson was Coroticus, whose soldiers were pilloried in a letter from St Patrick on account of their evil ways. They were 'not citizens of the holy Romans, but of the devil', he avowed, 'living in the enemy way of the barbarians.' For such a jibe to be meaningful, the Strathclyde Britons must have been aspiring to being Roman in the fifth century AD.

Gododdin emerged out of the old land of the Votadini, focused on the fertile Lothians, and extending to the Border counties. In Ayrshire lay Aeron. Stretching from Cumbria to Dumfries and Galloway was Rheged. Its focus was possibly the old Roman settlement at Carlisle, where it will be recalled Cuthbert was shown the town walls and a Roman fountain as late as 685.

By the time that these kingdoms had assumed coherent form, so too had the Anglo-Saxon settlements, and it was Rheged more than any other Scottish kingdom that was most closely concerned with the advance of the Angles of Northumbria. The Celts of Rheged fought their southern enemies with a ferocity which equalled that of the southern Britons in the fifth and sixth centuries.

Here, in sixth-century Rheged, arose Urien, a northern Arthur. Urien figures prominently in the poems attributed to Llywarch Hên, a Welshman who was his contemporary, but whose surviving poems seem to be mostly the work of a ninth-century imitator. The first cycle attributed to Llywarch tells of Urien's battles against the English, of the deeds of his sons, notably Owain, and of members of his court, including Llywarch himself and his fellow bard, Taliesin. The culmination of the cycle is a description of the death of Urien, the desolation of his court and the devastation left after his death. His head was carried off (an interesting survival of pagan Celtic custom), and a lament said over it which evokes the spirit of the age (translated by N. K. Chadwick, *Celtic Britain*, London, 1963, p. 107):

> A head I carry, close to my side
> Head of Urien, generous leader of hosts,
> And on his white breast, a black carrion crow.
> A head I hold up which once sustained me,
> My arm is numb, my body trembles,
> My heart breaks;
> This head I cherish, formerly cherished me.

This desolation is carried on from the description of his ruined stronghold – the hearth, once blazing away with logs heating cauldrons, is choked with weeds and overgrown with bugloss and dock. Falcon and hind have gone, and the whole landscape, once brilliantly lit by rushlights and echoing with the shouts of warriors, has been taken over by rooting pigs and pecking birds.

During his lifetime Urien kept the Anglian advance at bay, pushing the enemy back and laying siege to an island, Metcaud, perhaps Lindisfarne. On the accession of Aethelfrith of Bernicia the tide turned, and the Anglian annexation of lowland Scotland was put seriously in hand. At the battle

of Degsastan in 603 the Scottic king Aedan of Dalriada
joined forces with the Britons only to meet with defeat. The
east Lothians were now open to the Angles, and Rheged
was soon annexed also. Oswiu, king of Northumbria,
married the daughter of Urien to clinch the takeover.

The Angles pushed westwards, and by the late seventh
century had also gained control of the valley of the Clyde.
Gradually, however, they lost the lands they had conquered. In the tenth century much reverted to the control of
the king of a now unified Scotland, and in 1016 (or 1018) at
the battle of Carham king Malcolm II of Scotland won back
for the Celts the remaining land between Forth and Tweed
that had been held by the English.

The Scots

The Scots, who had started to settle during the Roman
period, and who gave Scotland her name, formed the Dark
Age kingdom of Dalriada. Later tradition claimed that the
colonization of western Scotland by the Scots took place
between about 490 and 500, when

> The three sons of Erc, son of Eochaidh, the valiant
> Three who had the blessing of Patrick
> Took Alban, increased their courage
> Loarn, Fergus and Angus.

A seventh- or eighth-century source claimed that 150 men
came with the three sons of Erc, led by Fergus. In all probability, however, the sons of Erc were not moving into unknown lands, and some Irish had been established in
Scotland before the royal line moved over to rule them.
Once in Scotland, they organized themselves in groups of
family origins.

The Scots probably met with little resistance. The areas
they settled were under-populated and, in terms of good
farm land, far from desirable. At once the Scots found themselves hemmed in: to the north and east lay the Picts, to the
south-west were the Britons. Under such circumstances,
there was only one thing to do, fight or be elbowed out. Not
in vain were they called Scots (the name means 'bandits').
They took up weapons and began their long but ultimately
victorious war against the Picts. By the ninth century, when
Kenneth mac Alpin king of the Scots united both peoples,
they had already given Scotland one great legacy apart from
her name – the Gaelic speech. In the days of Dalriada, the
language spoken in both Ireland and Scotland was Common
Gaelic. Only subsequently did Irish and Scots Gaelic
diverge. At first the language was confined to Dalriada, but
the activities of Irish monks from Iona in the territories of the

Picts had already resulted in Gaelic being known in Pictish lands before Kenneth mac Alpin came to the throne. From the union of the two peoples onwards, the language spread rapidly. By the eleventh century Gaelic was in use the length and breadth of Scotland, except for a narrow strip along the English border and in the Norse-speaking areas of the Hebrides and the Northern Isles.

The puzzle of the Picts

The Picts have long been a mystery. An Icelandic writer in the twelfth century said they were small men who did wonders in the mornings and evenings but who at mid-day lost their strength and had to hide away underground. In later ages they seemed almost as fabulous, and something of the mystery of the Picts has survived to haunt twentieth-century archaeologists and historians.

One reason for this was that they spoke a lost language which was in part Celtic but in part belonged to some more ancient tradition, perhaps the tongue spoken by the natives of the late Bronze Age in eastern Scotland. Like the other lost languages of ancient Europe (Etruscan, Minoan and Oscan), Pictish has disappeared by historical accident. When the Scots of Dalriada became the dominant force in the welding together of medieval Scotland, it was not in their interests to keep alive any Pictish traditions. Manuscripts were set down in Latin, and where earlier records were transcribed, those that were deemed worthy of preservation related to the Scots rather than to their enemies.

Furthermore, very few original manuscripts survive from the Dark Ages; most owe their preservation to having been transcribed by monks in the twelfth century or later. Anglo-Saxon documents survived because of twelfth-century antiquarian interest in their society. There was no such curiosity in the past in Scotland. Later generations did not improve the situation. When Edward I harried Scotland in the thirteenth-century Wars of Independence he took Scottish documents back to England, where in the fullness of time many were eaten by London rats. What Edward missed, the fanatical followers of John Knox and the Reformation set on fire when they devastated monasteries in the sixteenth century. All that remained on parchment was a king-list, and what is known of Pictish history must be pieced together from casual references in contemporary English and Irish writings.

Very few other clues survive to point to the nature of the Pictish language. They consist of the personal names of Pictish kings, a scatter of place-names and a few terse inscriptions on stone, bone and silver. Nevertheless, there is good reason to suppose that not only were the Picts literate, but that they kept a considerably body of records, perhaps in both the native tongue and the adopted Latin. Its loss is an irreparable tragedy to any study of the post-Roman Celts.

Pictish history begins with the career of Bridei mac Maelcon, who won a victory over Gabran of the Scots some time in the second half of the sixth century. This effectively put an end to a long period of conflict between Pict and Scot, and there was peace for about fifteen years. Bridei assumes reality in the writings of Adamnan, the biographer of St Columba. The saint made a journey to the Pictish court and there set in hand a campaign of conversion, though there is other evidence to suggest that some at least of the Picts were already Christian.

When Bridei died in 584 Pictland probably extended from the Orkneys in the north to Manau, part of Gododdin, in the south. With his death it is possible that the Orkneys rebelled against their Pictish overlords, and sought help from Dalriada. Whatever the case, Aedan mac Gabran, the Scottic king, found the occasion opportune for an invasion of Pictland. Since he had to contend with the Angles, who defeated him and his allies the Strathclyde Britons utterly at the battle of Degsastan, it is not certain whether he annexed Pictish territory. After this a veil descends on Pictish affairs until the second half of the seventh century, when the Angles again made an impact north of the Forth–Clyde line by annexing part of southern Pictland, perhaps the whole of the Mounth (part of the Grampians between the rivers Esk and Dee, Kincardineshire). They held their new territory until 685, when the Picts drove them out, following their victory at Nechtansmere (Angus) in that year.

In 706 Nechtan mac Derelei succeeded the Pictish throne. Unlike his predecessors Nechtan was pro-Anglian in out-look, and invited guidance from Northumbria on the method of calculating the date of Easter, a thorny problem to the Dark Age inhabitants of Britain. Northumbrian masons came to Pictland at this time, and the outcome was the building of a stone church, of which the tower still stands as part of the priory of Restenneth, Angus. Nechtan's reign ended in chaos, as three contestants claimed the throne. The victor was Oengus mac Fergus, a dynamic and highly competent soldier, who set about drumming the Scots out of Pictland and who carried the offensive first into Dalriada (and possibly Ireland) and then into Strathclyde. By 741 Oengus was effectively master of all that lay north of the Forth and Clyde. In the previous year an attempt had been

69 The 'Drosten' Stone, St Vigeans, Angus. The edge of this Class II Pictish cross-slab has an inscription 'Drosten ipe uoret et forcus' which is one of the very few inscriptions in the Pictish language to have survived (see also Plate 86a). Drosten and Forcus are personal names, Drosten being the same as Tristram. It dates probably from the eighth century

made by the Northumbrians to seize land in Pictland while Oengus was otherwise occupied, but he had come off the victor. His obsession with the conquest of Strathclyde led him to ally with anyone willing to support his cause, including the distant Cuthred of Wessex. Oengus died in 761, his objective unrealized.

The fortunes of war were to change several times, however, before destiny decreed that Dalriada and Pictland were to be fused into one kingdom. The driving force behind the unification was the Dalriadic Scottic king, Kenneth mac Alpin. The date of the union of Picts and Scots is not certain, because contemporary chroniclers were more concerned about the growing Viking threat at this time, but it is likely to have taken place in 849 or 850. The union was probably the outcome of a military campaign, and was followed up by the Scottish colonization of Pictland. From the middle of the ninth century the Picts ceased to exist as an independent nation, though something of their culture lingered on.

The wrath of the Vikings

'Deliver us O Lord from the wrath of the Vikings', wrote a demented monk in his monastery in Gaul at the end of the eighth century, at a time when the learning of Celtic monks from Ireland had been spread through Europe by missionaries. It was no hollow prayer, and the monks before all others had reason to be afraid, for the rich treasures accumulated in monasteries were the kind of booty the pagan raiders were out to scoop. Here were barbarians even fiercer than the Celts had been.

The Vikings comprised a motley collection of northerners. Although many of the raiding parties were composed of men of mixed origins, the Norse (from Norway, though the term is sometimes used to describe all the Vikings) were particularly active in Scotland and the Isle of Man, the Danes in England and the Swedes played more of a part in activities on the Continent than in Britain. Their coming transformed Celtic Britain. They first made their appearance in British history in 787, when the *Anglo-Saxon Chronicle* records a Viking raid on Northumbria. In 793 the Northumbrian monastery of Lindisfarne was sacked, and in the following year an attack on the monastery at Jarrow was repulsed. Early in the ninth century there were raids on the Scottish monastery of Iona.

Archaeological evidence suggests that these raids were not the beginning of the incursions but that they took place when Vikings were already establishing settlements in Scotland. By the tenth century the Norse were well established. They colonized the Northern and Western Isles and the north Scottish mainland, and took over the Isle of Man as a convenient jumping-off point for the coasts bordering the Irish Sea. Wales was subjected to raids, but was never colonized, except perhaps by a few families, but Cumbria, Lancashire and Cheshire suffered from immigrations of both Norse and Danes. Galloway was settled somewhat later by a fierce mixture of Irish-Norse known as the Gallghaideal.

In most of the areas in which the Vikings settled the population was relatively sparse, and there seems to have been little difficulty in absorbing them. In the Northern Isles they may even have adopted some of the Pictish building customs when they developed a regional variant of their distinctive longhouses. Norse rule in the north was to last into the full Middle Ages, and left its legacy for our own time – in Shetland a survival of Norse law permits salmon to be fished with a net, while northern fishermen still speak a dialect descended from that of the Vikings. So too in the Isle of Man, whose present parliament, the House of Keys, owes its origins to the Viking period.

Elsewhere the Viking legacy was not as long-lasting, but it was by no means negligible. The art of the British Isles, for long growing progressively moribund, was suddenly stimulated into vigorous life as Scandinavian monsters, patterns and characters from Norse mythology, took over the drab surfaces of late Celtic sculpture.

Celtic cowboys and craftsmen

How then did the population live in this new Celtic world where kings are known by name? The world had changed since the time when the Celts squabbled amongst themselves in the face of the Roman legions. The Celts outside the old Roman territory were becoming civilized by degrees: perhaps enforced by the terror of the Vikings, certainly by their adoption of Christianity (p. 151).

The rocky citadel of Dunadd in the heart of Argyllshire now rises above flat fields, its twin peaks thrown up in some primeval eruption. In the time of the Picts and Scots it was surrounded by bog. Dunadd above all other places in Dark Age Celtic Britain symbolizes the life of its age. This was an important citadel of the Scottic kings of Dalriada, recalling Iron Age hillforts yet differing from them.

The passing centuries had by the fifth century left their mark on the Celts even outside the areas which had come under the hand of Rome. Society was still tribal and heroic, but somehow the world had shrunk. The great tribes of the

Iron Age had become fragmented, new kingdoms had formed, and men followed the leader of their war-band, to whom they felt a personal tie.

It is possible that the population was smaller. Chronicles of the sixth century are full of tales of fearful plagues which left the city streets full of corpses the length and breadth of Europe, and it seems unlikely that these were entirely confined to Roman towns (p. 124). Maelgwn died of the yellow plague, after all, and Gildas tells how it was rife among the

70 Dunadd, Argyll. This rocky outcrop in the Crinan Moss (once surrounded by bog) was chosen by the Scottic (i.e. Irish) settlers in western Scotland for their capital when the kingdom of Dalriada was founded in the fifth century. It was occupied until the coming of the Norse, and is a 'nuclear' fort with a central citadel and outworks. It produced many finds when excavated at the beginning of this century

British around 550. It was the Celtic cosmopolitan outlook that probably resulted in its spread. Ships from the Continent regularly visited Celtic British shores, bringing imports of wine and pottery and returning with such merchandise as lead from Cornwall or the Severn Estuary. These ships brought not only luxuries but death. It might even have come straight from Egypt – Coptic beads and pottery have been found in Celtic Britain – and it spread fast. Alas for the Celts, it was to be a British disease. It does not seem to have afflicted the Anglo-Saxon immigrants too badly, if at all. At this period they had little or no direct contact with the Mediterranean world and it seems to have burnt out before reaching their Continental homelands. Thus trade between Saxons across the Channel was unaffected. No doubt the plague inhibited the contacts between Celts and Saxons that might otherwise have flourished. The scale of the plague was probably comparable to that of the Black Death in 1348. In the highland areas of Britain the population had never been vast: in the Dark Ages it was sparse. If a war leader wished to occupy a fort such as Maiden Castle it would have been a dream, for there were not enough men alive in any one area to man the Iron Age defences.

Thus reduced in numbers, the Celts lived on in their old haunts, slightly modifying their lifestyle to accord with social change. It is noteworthy that the hillforts re-occupied in the Roman period do not seem to have outlived the sixth century. The forts that were built new in the Dark Ages were in a new style. They are known to archaeologists as nuclear forts; the main element is a small inner citadel on a rocky

71 The Mote of Mark, Kirkcudbright. This small outcrop overlooking the Solway Firth on the edge of Dalbeattie Forest at Rockcliffe was first occupied in the fifth century when it was defended by a timber-laced rampart which subsequently vitrified. In the sixth to seventh century it was occupied by metalworkers, who made a variety of intricately decorated brooches and mounts for which the moulds, crucibles and other metalworking refuse were found in excavation in 1913 and 1973. There was evidence for its destruction in the seventh century, and for a hybrid Celtic-Anglian population there late in its occupation – a runic inscribed bone of Anglian origin was found there in 1973

outcrop, with a series of outer courtyards formed by linking sections of outcrop with walling. Dunadd is a classic example of this, first occupied perhaps in the early sixth century. References in literary sources allude to it in the seventh century and finds show it was still inhabited on the arrival of the Vikings in the ninth.

In such nuclear forts the chief (in the case of Dunadd, probably the king) lived with his family and immediate followers in the inner citadel, the outer enclosures reserved for work and possibly stock compounds. For the Dark Age Celts were above all stock raisers. The bones found at Dunadd and Dinas Powys, Glamorgan, showed that the most popular meat was pork. Dinas Powys could have been a royal site, like Dunadd. Other bones from these sites and the Mote of Mark, Kirkcudbrightshire, include dog skeletons and gnawed bones, showing that domestic pets were kept, perhaps to help in hunting. Deer were also represented on all three sites by bone and antler.

Arable farming played a secondary role. The querns for grinding grain were ubiquitous at Dunadd, but at both Dinas Powys and the Mote of Mark they were very few in number. Fields, however, tilled in the post-Roman period, have been excavated at Gwithian in Cornwall, and at Dinas Emrys in Gwynedd there are signs that field systems were cultivated on the lower slopes of the hill on which the fort once stood, though whether these are contemporary with its Dark Age occupation is not provable.

One very distinctive feature of the Celtic Dark Age sites in Britain is the variety of industries carried out in them. Iron, bronze and lead were wrought and cast while bone and

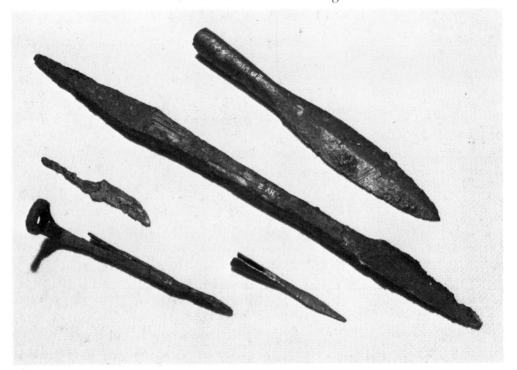

72 Iron objects from Buston crannog, Ayrshire, a lake dwelling on an artificial island occupied in the seventh century AD. From top right to bottom left the objects are a spearhead, a spoonbit for woodworking, a knife, an arrowhead and the bit from a barrel padlock

stone were fashioned into a diverse assemblage of objects. The Dark Age Celts had inherited Roman and Iron Age legacies in their metallurgical skills. The carburizing of iron to form a 'steel' was not unknown to them though it is doubtful that this process was entirely deliberate. To the Roman inheritance must go the credit of introducing new types of copper alloys, notably the adding of zinc to copper to produce brass. Plating bronze with a thin wash of silver may also have been an Imperial survival.

While many of the possessions of the Dark Age Celts are very similar to those made and used by their Iron Age forebears, many others show the influence of Roman prototypes. This is particularly true of some iron tools – barrel padlocks and keys, hammers, axes and so on. It is also true of a wide variety of objects of personal adornment, ranging from different types of bronze and bone pins and brooches through melon-shaped beads to combs made out of riveted plates of bone.

Roman survival did not extend to pottery. While some Roman pottery was still used in what was once the province of Britannia, and was even imitated locally, for example at Gwithian in Cornwall, the collapse of the Roman commercial pottery industry meant that mass-produced pottery was a thing of the past by the late fifth century. No native

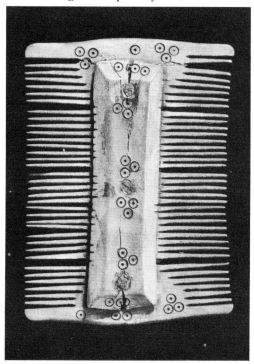

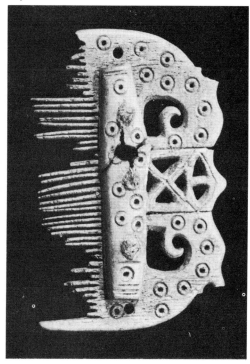

pottery was produced to replace it, except perhaps in a few remote areas where long-surviving Iron Age traditions of potting seem to have persisted untouched by Roman innovations, as in parts of north Wales and the Western and Northern Isles of Scotland. For most people wood and leather provided acceptable alternatives, as they did for many of the domestic needs of later medieval Britain. The lucky few, however, were able to import ware to suit their needs.

Imported pottery is the surviving archaeological evidence for what must have been a vigorous overseas trade. There are many types of imports – *mortaria* (mixing and grinding bowls) from the region round Bordeaux, and later a variety of bowls, jugs and other vessels from the same area represent just one channel of trade. Some of this traffic had begun

73 (*Left*) Bone comb, Buston crannog, Ayrshire. This is typical of the composite bone combs popular in the Dark Ages. The type is of Romano-British origin, as is the ring-and-dot ornament. Combs seem to have had a special significance for both Celts and Saxons in the Dark Ages. Seventh century

74 (*Right*) Bone comb, Dun Cuier, Barra. This single-edged composite comb has a pair of confronted but stylized animals. It came from a stone-walled fort

147

75 Pottery from Tintagel, Cornwall. The sherds on the left are of what has been termed 'A' ware, a type of red-slip pottery produced in North Africa in the late-Roman and post-Roman period. At the bottom left can be seen one sherd stamped with a cross. The sherds on the right are of 'B' ware – amphorae and jugs usually in creamy-buff ware which were also imported to Britain from the eastern Mediterranean in the fifth century. Such imports are important for dating Dark Age Celtic sites. Tintagel may have been a trading settlement later adapted to monastic use

well within the Roman occupation. Red-slipped bowls from North African kilns had reached South Shields near Hadrian's Wall as early as the second century, and in the fourth century red-slipped bowls of very similar type to those imported in the fifth had come in to centres like London as well as to western forts like Lancaster. From the eastern Mediterranean too came amphorae in a variety of colours loaded no doubt with wine and other commodities, perhaps, as one recent commentator has punned, 'Dark Age dates'. Some of this pottery was decorated with stamped ornament which may have contributed to the development of contemporary art; other subjects, such as the pottery pilgrim's flasks decorated with representations of St Menas which came from his shrine in Alexandria, or embroidered textiles also from Egypt, may have similarly played a part in the dissemination of new art motifs.

Internal trade was not as vigorous as that with far-off lands. In the absence of hillfort markets, most communities seem to have been largely self-sufficient, confining their barter to a limited area. Travelling craftsmen and salesmen, however, must have been as commonplace as in the earlier

Iron Age, and indeed the clay moulds and other evidence for ornamental metalworking that turn up on a high percentage of Dark Age Celtic sites may well have been the refuse left by an itinerant smith. There is no doubt that either by trade or by travellers from more distant parts bringing new concepts to the community, there was a fairly rapid spread of ideas in the Celtic world of the fifth and sixth centuries, slowing down later with a corresponding growing of parochialism in art and culture. But even peoples as apparently hostile as Picts and Scots borrowed from one another. Irish motifs appeared in Pictland and Pictish brooches turned up in Ireland, having passed, no doubt, through Dalriada. Now and again it is possible to point to a more far-flung but still organized trade, for example in armlets of Yorkshire jet which appear in far-flung corners of the Celtic realms, but such instances are rare.

What had happened to the warriors? The number of fighting men was small by Iron Age standards, but the Celts did their best to keep up their reputation for recklessness in battle. The use of horses without chariots had been seen at its best in the Roman cavalry but Iron Age Celts rode too. Horses were an essential element in Dark Age Celtic warfare, but organized cavalry charges seem from the evidence of contemporary poetry to have been of little consequence in tactics, which reverted to a more haphazard charging and flinging of spears.

76 Sherd of a stamped lamp from Dinas Emrys, Gwynedd (see Plate 59), which was probably imported from the eastern Mediterranean, and is in a ware related to 'A' ware. The stamp is the Chi-Rho (the sacred monogram of Christ) between alpha and omega ('I am the beginning and the end'). It is likely that trade with the eastern Mediterranean also helped foster Christianity in fifth-century Celtic Britain

77 A beaker of 'E' ware from Buston crannog, Ayrshire. Seventh century. 'E' ware is a gritty, grey or buff pottery which is common on Celtic sites of the sixth and later centuries down to the Viking raids. It has been suggested that it was imported from the Bordeaux region, but it cannot be matched there in surviving pots (the clay is like that of the Bordeaux region) and it is not impossible that it was made somewhere in Britain. This characteristic vessel is known as a 'Buston Beaker'

149

Horsemen, either warrior or huntsmen, abound in Pictish sculptures, which show mounted Picts using saddle cloths and reins. Part of a bit has been found at the Mote of Mark and bronze harness fittings come from various parts of Pictland. Spears are the principal weapons carried on the sculptures, and actual spearheads have been found at Dunadd and at Buston in Ayrshire. Swords are sometimes depicted, with pommels reminiscent of those found in pagan Saxon England, though actual swords are only re-

78 *(Left)* A Pictish horseman adorns this slab from Meigle, Perthshire. It is one of the large collection of stones from this site. Notice the scabbard chape of St Ninian's Isle type (see Plate 86a), the saddlecloth and spear. The other side carries a cross. Eighth century

79 *(Right)* A drinking Pict adorns this slab from Inver-gowrie, Angus. Notice again the bridle, and the drinking horn with bird's-head terminal, reminiscent of both the heads on the horns from Torrs (Plate 8) and those on the Saxon drinking horns from Taplow. Notice too the tiny round targe-like shield

presented by possible fragments from Dunadd. Bows and arrows also made their appearance in Pictish sculptures. Absent in the Iron Age, these, like the form of some of the spearheads, perhaps owe their origin to auxiliaries in the Roman army. An arrow was found at Buston, and another came from Dunadd.

The Dark Age warrior seems to have had little for pro-tection. The shields represented in Pictish sculpture are either small round targes, or equally small rectangular boards with a central boss, that were probably adapted from

Roman *scutum* shields, some time in the early centuries AD,
in northern Britain.

At the end of the day the warrior could relax in his lord's hall. A sculpture from Ivergowrie, Angus, shows a Pict quaffing from a drinking horn with a bird's-head terminal mount. Could it be he is celebrating with the whisky, which Scottish folklore claims was the invention of a Pict?

The men of God

During the centuries in which Pictish, Scottish, British and Welsh culture was flourishing, Britain had become Christian. Of all the influences to mould the development of Celtic society, none had greater impact than the Christian faith. Once received by the Celts, the new belief was translated into forms which were distinctively Celtic. The lives of the early saints embody all the virtues of the pastoral side of the Church: the image of the gentle hermit disdaining all possessions and living a life of service to God, in a humble cell, is one of the most powerful in the history of the Church. The early saints attained what later mystics strove towards – they were simple men whose humility and integrity shows through the embroidered accounts of their biographers.

The Celtic Church is usually thought of as monastic, but it was not always so. Christianity probably first took root in the western and northern parts of Britain during the Roman period, possibly introduced by the army. Hadrian's Wall was one region in which various cults flourished, and there can be little doubt that Christianity was here well established before the end of the fourth century. In Wales, too, the Faith was probably brought by the army. By the fourth century a diocesan structure was set up in Britain. It is not impossible that the *Praefecti Gentium* sent to administer the emergent kingdoms of Dark Age Britain also had a hand in the spread of Christianity, and in the setting up of some kind of diocesan structure in their areas. Certainly by the fifth century there is evidence from tombstones that the Church in Scotland and less certainly Wales was organized into dioceses, presided over by bishops and deacons. Saints Ninian and Patrick were both described by their biographers as bishops, and Gildas wrote about the Church of his own day as though it were diocesan.

This structure probably persisted until the seventh century, by which time monasticism was growing in popularity. Monastic organization was better suited to the Celtic Church than diocesan, since dioceses were devised in the Roman Empire where Christianity was urban-based. The Celts had no towns, and their society was tribal. From the outset, therefore, the administration had to be adapted to suit a different world, and it would seem logical to suppose that the centres were initially either the surviving Roman forts or other foci of the new kingdoms.

Tombstones provide most information about the early Celtic Church, and point to links with the Continent in the fifth and sixth centuries. The stones are upright pillars, usually undressed, with horizontal inscriptions in Roman capitals giving the name of the deceased and usually that of his father. They are most densely concentrated in Wales, but an appreciable number are to be found in Cornwall, and yet others are scattered through lowland Scotland.

The names of these long-forgotten Celts are mostly Roman (p. 131), and reflect changing Continental fashion. The presence of such names as Paulinus, Salvian, Honoratus, Avitus, Severinus, Victor and Vitalis on the stones show that the names fashionable in Britain were those popular in contemporary Gaul. Melus the doctor buried in Gwynedd had a father called Martinus, almost certainly named after St Martin of Tours, as until his time the name was relatively uncommon in the Roman world. Some formulae, such as the simple 'Memoria' ('In memory of') have their counterparts in North Africa, others like the ubiquitous 'Hic iacit' ('Here lies') stones seem to originate in Gaul. Sometimes the Continental link is even more apparent, as on one of the stones from Penmachno, Gwynedd, which was set up 'in tempore consule Justine' ('in the time of the consul Justinus') – Justinus is only mentioned on memorials from the Lyons region, and lived around 540.

One feature of the memorial stones that was not of Mediterranean inspiration was the custom of naming the father of the deceased. This practice, frowned on in Continental Europe because it seemed to flaunt the order of Matthew 23:9, 'Call no man your father upon the earth', stemmed from Celtic tribal society with its emphasis on the role of the father, and was too much for orthodoxy. The heresy probably began in Ireland, where stones were inscribed in the native Ogham alphabet with the traditional formula 'A maqqi B' ('A son of B') – the Latin inscribed stones of western Britain may be due to the influence of Irish settlers.

The enduring nature of Celtic tradition shows through not only in the formulae used on tombstones, but even in more fundamental matters such as the shape and siting of graveyards. In Celtic Britain the places of the gods had always been demarcated by a circular enclosure. It was the sacred

circle: it separated the holy from the profane and the dead from the living. The priests of the Neolithic farmers, perhaps the first 'druids', set out their henges with bank and ditch enclosing a circle. So too the builders of the Bronze Age circles of standing stones such as Stonehenge. In the Iron Age, though some temples may have been rectilinear, there was still a marked preference for circular enclosures, and the tradition did not die out during the Roman occupation. Circular enclosures delimited burials at Camerton and Leighton Buzzard, and there was a tendency to favour circular plans for Romano-Celtic temples, for example at Brigstock, Winterton or Housesteads. Of the Celtic Christian cemeteries that were enclosed, the delimiting bank or wall was circular, and circular churchyards were to persist into the Middle Ages and beyond. The older churchyards of north Wales or northern Scotland are still circular today; though the wall may be a modern fabrication, it frequently overrides the mound of its medieval precursor.

A conservatism more remarkable than that displayed in the plan of churchyards can be detected in the choice of sites. Few early graveyards have been investigated scientifically, but where they have there have frequently been indications that the site had been previously used for pagan interments. In some cases this may have been fortuitous, but it can hardly have always been so. The cemetery of oriented Christian burials at St Ninian's Point, Bute, seems to have followed in unbroken succession from a cemetery of disoriented, and therefore presumably pagan, graves. At

80 (*Left*) The Latinus Stone Whithorn. This fifth-century memorial stone is one of the earliest in Dark Age Britain, and is incised in good Roman letters – its models are Roman. Its inscription reads TE DOMINU(m) LAUDAMUS LATINUS ANNORU(m) XXXV ET FILIA SUA ANN(orum) IV (h)IC SI(g)NUM FECERUNT NEPUS BARROVADI.

81 (*Centre*) One of three stones from Penmachno, Gwynedd. The inscription reads FILI AVITORI IN TE(m)PO(re) IVSTI(ni) CON(sulis). This commemorates Avitorius, and notes that it was set up in the time of the consul Justinus, whose name appears only in the Vienne district of France and who is known to have been consul in 540.

82 (*Right*) A memorial stone from Aberdaron, Gwynedd, dating from the late fifth or early sixth century. It commemorates Senacus, described as a 'presbyter' buried with a multitude of his brethren. It is evidence for a diocesan organization of the Church in Wales at this time

153

Ancaster, Lincolnshire, a late Roman Christian cemetery was found to take over from an earlier pagan use, pagan slabs from a shrine being trimmed and re-used as cover stones for graves. In the Isle of Man even older sites were used.

There are other hints of ancient Celtic traditions carried into the Dark Ages. The very shape of some fifth- and early sixth-century memorial stones recall more ancient standing stones, and indeed it is not impossible that some were re-used prehistoric menhirs. In Wales a classic example is provided by the series of four stones, perhaps part of a processional way, which stand in the churchyard at Gwytherin. One was re-used in the fifth century, and has an added inscription proclaiming that it was erected to Vinnemaglus, son of Sennemaglus.

The very form of the graves harks back to bygone days. Some were simple affairs, hollows dug out of the living rock or soil, but others were more elaborate, constructed of slabs of stone set in the ground to form boxes or cists. Cist burial is a phenomenon of the Celtic Iron Age, when the mortal remains of the dead in northern Britain were interred in small stone boxes. The Dark Age cists are larger, the increase in dimensions being dictated by change in burial custom, but are firmly rooted in the same tradition.

Amazingly, there were still druids in fifth-century Britain. In the *Life of St Brigit* we are informed she was brought up in the house of a druid, and another source asserts she was the daughter of one. St Mochta of Louth's parents were the slaves of a British druid, according to his biographer. No traditions are stronger than those of the Elder Faiths.

Churches

The first churches built in Celtic Britain recall in many ways pagan Celtic temples. The tradition universal in the Roman Empire was one of stone-built churches, their basilican plan based on the public buildings of cities. Some, like the Roman church excavated at Silchester, Hants, were modest by imperial standards, but all the right ingredients were there – a nave flanked by side aisles, a narthex and a semi-circular apse. This was the model followed by St Augustine when he came to reinforce Christianity in Anglo-Saxon Kent, and which was to remain, with variations, the ideal of Anglo-Saxon builders. Not so among the Celts. The stone building, seen to be synonymous with Rome in the minds of the Saxon architects, was rejected for timber, with room for little more than the officiating priest. Architecturally they are less accomplished than the similar Celtic Iron Age temples at

Heathrow and South Cadbury. If there were grander buildings, none are known. The flimsy nature of these early chapels has meant that they have seldom come to light. In Britain only two have been discovered, beneath later stone buildings at Ardwall Isle, Kirkcudbright, and Burryholms, Glamorgan, and even these may not date from as early as the sixth or seventh century.

Almost as few stone churches survive outside Ireland. Stone building came late to the Celts, for whom resistance to Roman architecture seems to have become equated with resistance to Roman Christianity. It is not impossible that what eventually drove the Celts to build in stone was the threat of Viking attacks, for timber chapels were particularly vulnerable to devastation by fire. In Ireland the first stone buildings make their appearance around the end of the eighth century, and Scotland may have soon followed its example, the first essays in stone architecture following the arrival of Northumbrian masons in Pictland in the time of Nechtan mac Derelei. These would have been exceptional, and the stone grassed-over footings of unicameral chapels that can be detected in many parts of Scotland and the Isle of Man all belong probably to the tenth and later centuries. Apart from the tower at Restenneth, Angus, and another tower in very late Saxon style at St Andrews, Fife, which may in fact post-date the Norman Conquest, only two ecclesiastical buildings survive in any measure intact from Celtic Britain. These are both round towers, built in Irish style at Abernethy, Perthshire, and Brechin, Angus, following the Irish infiltration of Pictland in the ninth and later centuries. Even these are late, both probably put up in the tenth or eleventh century.

83 (*Left*) Spooyt Vane Keeill, Michael, Isle of Man. This particularly picturesque chapel site is typical of very many to be found in the Isle of Man. The chapel is a simple, unicameral building of which the foundations only survive, set within an enclosure, with a rectangular priest's cell at one corner. Most probably belong to the eighth century and later – some may be medieval

84 (*Right*) Round tower, Abernethy, Perthshire. Detached round towers are a feature of Irish ecclesiastical architecture of the Viking Age and later, but only two examples survive in Scotland, this and one at Brechin, Angus. It is one of the few surviving examples of pre-Norman architecture in Scotland, and shows features of Anglo-Saxon architecture. Probably tenth century, partly rebuilt in the eleventh

Monasticism – the triumph of the Celtic Church

Monasticism was an innovation from the eastern Mediterranean, and there is little evidence that it took any real hold in Britain before the sixth century. The complex at Tintagel, Cornwall, once believed to be that of a fifth-century monastery, is now probably to be interpreted as a secular settlement, though it may have become monastic later. The first monasteries may have been established in Wales a little before AD 500; by the sixth century the move-

85 Tintagel, Cornwall. This rocky peninsula is one of the most famous sites of Dark Age Britain, and is steeped in Arthurian lore. The dominant remains are of a medieval castle, but on the 'island' can be seen the foundations of rectangular buildings which have been identified as the cells of an early monastery. There is some doubt as to whether the site was monastic from the outset, and it is without exact parallel. The photograph shows (*right*) the foundations of Site B. The wall (*bottom left*) is the 'iron gate', part of the medieval castle. For imported Mediterranean pottery found here, see Plate 75. According to legend, Tintagel was the birthplace of king Arthur

ment had spread to Ireland and by the late sixth century to northern Britain. It was taken up by the Northumbrians from their Celtic predecessors in the seventh. The first monasteries may have been set within rectilinear enclosures – this is the case at Iona in Scotland – and it has been suggested that this follows the plan of eastern monasteries, whose prototypes were Roman forts. A more local inspiration is just as likely, for the forts of Roman Britain still survived in the late fifth century and it is notable that some were re-used for early monasteries – Celtic foundations grew up within the walls of Caer Gybi of Holyhead and Burgh Castle in Norfolk, the latter the outcome of an Irish missionary expedition led by St Fursa. Whether local or oriental, the rectilinear enclosures were short-lived, and soon Celtic monasteries, like Celtic grave-yards, were protected by circular enclosures. They bore no similarity to what is now thought of as a monastery, with cloister, chapter house, dorter and other ranges carefully deployed according to a plan. Such claustral monasteries were the outcome of monastic reform in later centuries, and were not disseminated in Britain before the eleventh and twelfth centuries. Celtic foundations were eremitic – the word has the same root as 'hermit' – and comprised clusters of circular or rectilinear cells, chapels and subsidiary buildings such as 'schoolrooms' scattered about in a fairly haphazard fashion. They were the hub of economic units, the nearest the Celts ever got before the coming of the Vikings to an urban community. They had attendant communities of lay craftsmen and others who played their part in maintaining the life of the monastery.

Larger monasteries had smaller dependent offshoots, and smaller still, the hermitages with their single cell and chapel in a graveyard represent the reduction of the monastic ideal to the individual need. For those early clerics for whom even a hermitage seemed too materialistic a lifestyle, there were caves which could be inhabited, such as that associated with St Ninian at Physgyll in Galloway, or that of St Molaise on Arran.

The monasteries, great and small, kept learning alive, and played their part in the economy of the Celtic world. Their leaders were saints, but to become one required less rigorous means tests than have been applied to more recent men of God. All that was needed was a love of God and an ability to write, and that indeed is what the early saints did. They wrote not merely of the works of their Church, but also of the deeds of the secular world in which they lived, and the affairs of pagan worlds long dead. It was the learning of Dark Age monks that led them to transcribe pagan Celtic tales, and it is to them we owe our few glimpses of more ancient traditions.

Art

One day in 1958 a boy trying to relieve the boredom of his school holidays by assisting excavators unearth a little medieval chapel on St Ninian's Isle in Shetland uncovered one of the greatest collections of treasures that has ever come to light in British soil.

The St Ninian's Isle Treasure is superb. In its rich silverwork the art of the Celtic smith can be seen at its apogee, the mature distillation of centuries of experimentation and innovation.

The hoard was deposited around the year 800 in a larchwood box under the floor of the tiny church, probably to protect it from the pillaging hands of Vikings. Except for one piece, a magnificent silver hanging bowl which some have seen as being perhaps of Northumbrian manufacture, all the objects of which it is composed were made in a Pictish workshop or workshops in the eighth century. In all, the

86 Objects from the St Ninian's Isle Treasure, a hoard of Pictish silverwork found during the excavation of a chapel on a tidal islet off the coast of Shetland in 1958. Deposited around AD 800, perhaps in fear of the Viking raids, it is the finest collection of Celtic metalwork from the British Isles. The objects shown here are (a) scabbard chape with characteristically Pictish snub-snouted animals on the terminals, and an inscription in 'Irish' lettering but of Pictish words 'RESADFILISPUSSCIO' (i.e. probably 'Resad son of Spusscio', both Pictish names); (b) a group of 'pepperpots' of uncertain function, perhaps strap distributors for a sword harness, executed in a 'chip-carved' technique (notice again the snub-nosed animals, the use of shoulder spirals, and the continuing use of triskele ornament on the example on the far right, reminiscent of a hanging-bowl escutcheon); (c) a silver hanging bowl, the only surviving example, though a lost one is recorded as being found in the river Witham, Lincolnshire – this has been claimed as Northumbrian rather than Pictish, and as being older than the other objects (late seventh–early eighth century), but not on strong evidence

(a)

(b)

(c)

collection was composed of 28 items: apart from the hanging bowl there were 7 other bowls, 2 sword chapes, 3 pepperpot-shaped objects which may have been from a sword harness, a sword pommel, a spoon, and a single-pronged claw-shaped implement perhaps for eating shellfish. All these objects were silver, as were 12 penan-nular brooches. One object did not fit in with the splendour of the rest of the hoard – the jawbone of a porpoise.

The objects in the St Ninian's Isle hoard epitomize the eclecticism of Celtic Christian art. Consider for example the three pepperpots. The one, with its use of triskele patterns, spirals and *yin-yangs*, has a respectable ancestry which can be traced back through the ornament of the fifth and sixth centuries in Celtic Britain to the Roman period and before then into the Iron Age. The second pepperpot is in a different tradition. On one side it carries an interlaced pattern in sharp relief. There is no interlace in Iron Age Celtic art – this type of ornament started in the Roman world and was disseminated in Europe in the sixth and seventh centuries. The method of its execution on this chape is a technique known as 'pseudo-chip carving', devised not by the Celts but by the Germanic peoples of the Migration period. In the form in which it appears on the pepperpot, however, it has already been given new expression in Irish guise. The beasts which adorn this and the third pepperpot are of more complex ancestry still. There is nothing like them in either Iron Age or Roman art. Their shoulder spirals hint at some ultimate origin in the world of the Russian nomads, but their convoluted bodies are Germanic, and hark back to Anglo-Saxon beasts. The way in which their bodies are hatched is reminiscent of similar Irish ornament, and creatures quite like them can be found in manuscripts both in Northumbria and Ireland. Their heads, however, are distinctive. These, with their snub snouts segmented off from the rest of their faces, are peculiarly Pictish; such beasts are quite absent in English art. In these three objects is revealed a tangled story of borrowing and re-borrowing, in which elements developed in one society have been taken up and elaborated in another, only to return in a new guise to their homeland.

The art of the Dark Age Celts is as complex as that of their Iron Age forebears, as full of surprises and as exuberant as the finest products of Belgic workshops. Yet, although the spirit is close to that of La Tène art, the driving force which provides the immediate impetus is different. Dark Age artists were looking back less to an Iron Age past than to a Romano-British heritage. The fact that this encompassed elements which were ultimately of Iron Age origin was

(a)

(b)

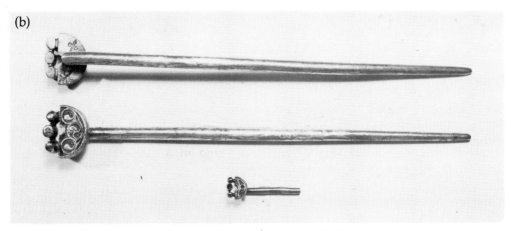

87 The beginnings of Dark Age Celtic art. This silver pin (a) was found at Oldcroft, Gloucestershire, in 1972 along with a hoard of around 3,330 Roman coins, which was deposited sometime between AD 354 and 359. The pin is of a type known as a proto-hand-pin. The plate is enamelled, and decorated with an eyed pelta and C-scrolls. Part of another pin of similar type was found out of context in a Roman villa at Atworth, Somerset. Such pins developed into hand-pins proper in the early Christian period. (b) A group from Norrie's Law, Fife, which formed part of a hoard of early Pictish silverwork (see Plate 102). The beads on the proto-hand-pin have now turned into 'fingers', and the design on the plate has become more ornate. Note the Pictish symbol on the back of the pin at the top. The date of the deposition of the Norrie's Law hoard is in dispute, but it is probably of the late sixth century

fortunate but coincidental: La Tène motifs were given a new lease of life in the Dark Ages not because they were Celtic but because they fitted in with barbarian Dark Age taste. It is noteworthy that all the basic elements of British art in the fifth and sixth centuries stemmed from the traditions of Roman Britain. The swirling triskeles that trick the eye into thinking them in giddy motion first delighted the wearers of Roman disc brooches, and were hung in openwork from the jangling harness of Roman horses in the far-flung corners of the Empire. The peltas that mushroom like bomb explosions on Dark Age metalwork were Roman representations of shields, viewed side on, while the intertwining of geometric interlace which was to adorn metal, stone and parchment alike· were long previously seen snaking across Roman mosaics like some complex exercise copied from a boy scout's knot-tying manual. The other patterns too had their genesis in the sweaty heat of Roman workshops – trumpet patterns, spirals, bead-and-reel and a host of other designs were woven by craftsmen familiar with barbarian tastes in the bewildering variety of metalwork designs turned out when Rome ruled the world.

The very objects on which this Dark Age ornament appear are Roman in origin. Nowhere are they to be seen better displayed than on hanging bowls, mysterious bronze vessels furnished with three suspension loops fastened

(a)

(b)

through ornamented escutcheons, the loops of which took the form of animal heads. Such hanging bowls first appear in fourth-century Roman Britain – one was found in a fourth-century hoard unearthed at Water Newton in 1975 – and were furnished at first with plain escutcheons or escutcheons made from the openwork popular with the late Roman army. The ornament was simple, consisting of the type of pelta pattern that was often favoured on harness pendants. A single pelta formed an escutcheon from Eastry, decorated with a very Roman trellis pattern, such as can be found on fourth-century coarse pottery, and stamped rosettes like those on similarly fourth-century New Forest ware. On some escutcheons enamelling was used, another Roman device given vogue on animal-shaped brooches much beloved of the soldiers on Hadrian's Wall. The ubiquitous design of these enamelled escutcheons was a triskele, ultimately of Iron Age origin but found too on disc brooches and other metalwork throughout the Roman period. Conceived in an Iron Age mind, and given birth in a Romano-British workshop, these triskeles, almost un-altered, later adorned the pages of manuscripts painted in monastic scriptoria.

Hanging bowls were one of the products of Dark Age workshops, in fashion from the fourth to the seventh century and possibly later. Another were the penannular brooches. These simple dress fasteners comprised a hoop of bronze, broken at one point to allow a pin to pass through cloth and swivel round on its loop. In origin they were Iron Age, popular with the Belgic Britons, but the Romano-Britons had adopted them to their own use and developed them ornamentally by pinching over the ends of the hoop and giving them the semblance of a snake's head.

88 More beginnings of Dark Age Celtic art. This disc brooch from Silchester, Hampshire (a) is one of a series of such brooches from Roman Britain which uses a triskele as a main motif – here it is composed of trumpet patterns. Such disc brooches were current from the second to the fourth century AD. Diameter: 4.1 cm approx. (b) An enamelled hanging-bowl escutcheon from Middleton Moor, Derbyshire, which like many such hanging-bowl escutcheons uses a triskele as a motif. Hanging bowls represent a survival from Roman Britain, and the art displayed on their escutcheons (which held the suspension chains) is of late Roman origin. The Middleton Moor find, which is enamelled in red, dates probably from the seventh century and came from a supposed Anglo-Saxon burial

161

89 Silvered bronze penannular brooch, Pant-y-Saer, Anglesey. This came from an enclosed hut group that seems to have been in use in the sixth century. The flaring terminals evolved out of earlier Romano-British types of penannular brooch, and were developed in some of the very ornate brooches of the seventh and eighth centuries

In Dark Age Britain penannular brooches proliferated until they are now fodder for a typologist's day dream. Whichever way they are grouped and dated, there is no doubt at all that most of the types popular in the Dark Ages were first made in Romano-British workshops, and the simple ornament with which they are sometimes decorated can be seen to have a similarly Roman origin. Later, under the artistic influence of the Anglo-Saxons, they were developed in Ireland and Scotland into magnificent pieces of jewellery, with huge expanded terminals ornamented with inlays and with the gold filigree so beloved of pagan Saxon craftsmen. These vast brooches, of which the Irish Tara Brooch and the Scottish Hunterston Brooch are outstanding examples, are among the finest achievements of Dark Age

90 The Hunterston Brooch, Ayrshire. This superb example of Celtic craftsmanship is modelled on earlier true penannular brooches, such as that in Plate 89, but the terminals have been joined to give greater rigidity. It is decorated with gold, silver and amber insets, and is of solid silver. It was probably made by an Anglo-Saxon craftsman working for a Celtic patron around AD 700, and is the earliest of a series of ornate brooches. Diameter (max.): 12.2 cm

Celtic art (though it has been suggested that the Hunterston Brooch was produced not by Celts, but by Anglo-Saxons catering for a Celtic market).

Pins too were a vehicle of Dark Age Celtic art. In Roman Britain various types of long pin, reminiscent of hat pins, were used to fasten clothing and anchor wayward hair, and these remained in vogue in later centuries. Some were of purely Roman design, but others, such as the hand-pins popular in Scotland and Ireland in the sixth and seventh centuries, represent Dark Age developments out of Roman types.

During the fifth and sixth centuries Celtic art remained firmly rooted in its Romano-British past. By the seventh century new ideas were making themselves felt. The Anglo-Saxons had introduced to Britain a host of new motifs and techniques – chip carving, granular and filigree work in gold, cloisonné inlays – and these were taken up by the Celts in Ireland and to a lesser extent Scotland. For some reason Wales and Cornwall stagnated artistically and contented themselves with dreary sculpture. Perhaps through Northumbria the Anglo-Saxons came into fruitful contact with both the Irish and the Picts, and ideas passed between the three peoples rapidly.

Until the seventh century Dark Age Celtic art had been the art of Christians, but not Christian art. Two centuries of contact with the Mediterranean had fostered a familiarity with the artistic traditions of this area. Some of the imported pottery from North Africa came stamped with Christian motifs, and others were no doubt introduced to Celtic Britain on imported textiles and in manuscripts. The outcome of such stimulus was new elements in Celtic art, borrowed directly from the Mediterranean world, or, occasionally, via Anglo-Saxon England. From now on this composite art was displayed in sculpture. No doubt there were wood carvings, textiles and decorated manuscripts also, but these have not survived, except for a few rare pieces which hint at tragic losses. Outside Scotland, ornamental metalwork does not seem to have been produced in Celtic Britain after the sixth century, or if it was, it has not survived. In Ireland the tradition flourished in the service of the Church, and, despite Viking looting, has left a wealth of reliquaries, brooches, book mounts and other objects to delight modern eyes. Manuscripts, so often regarded as the supreme medium of Dark Age Celtic artists, were mainly the product of the Anglo-Saxons and the Irish. As we shall see, there is good reason to believe the Picts were as skilled at manuscript illumination as they were as smiths and

91 (*Left*) Clay mould for casting an interlace-decorated roundel, Mote of Mark, Kirkcudbright. The Mote of Mark was a flourishing centre of metalworking in the sixth and seventh centuries. This mould, found in 1973, was perhaps for a circular mount for attaching to horse harness

sculptors, but the circumstances of history have robbed us of their creations. In Wales a few manuscripts were produced, but nothing has survived that is worth looking at twice from an artistic standpoint.

In Scotland Celtic art carried on an illuminating dialogue with Ireland. Among the Britons, ornamental metalworking enjoyed a brief flowering in the sixth and seventh centuries in the south-west, where a 'factory' for producing a variety of brooches, mounts and other objects has been excavated at

92 (*Right*) Reconstruction of the appearance of the design of a mount cast from a mould found at the Mote of Mark in 1913. Like Plate 91, it dates from the late sixth–early seventh century, and can be compared with some Anglo-Saxon phalerae of the later seventh century

the Mote of Mark in Kirkcudbright. Here Anglo-Saxon influence may have made its impact before this British art was destroyed by the Anglian advance around the mid-seventh century. At the Mote of Mark a rich diversity of clay moulds has been found for casting objects decorated with the usual repertoire of sixth-century Celtic motifs along with more exotic interlace, perhaps introduced directly from the Mediterranean. Bronze, brass, gold and perhaps lead were all worked in this tiny fortress on the Solway coast, and Germanic glass was imported, probably to make inlays and enamel.

There are links between the Mote of Mark and Ulster in so far as similar brooches and pins were popular on either side of the Irish Sea; similar links between Ireland and Scotland were maintained through Dalriada. Through Dalriada types of Pictish brooches probably reached Ireland, and Irish brooches came to influence Pictland. The Breadalbane Brooch, named after its collector Lord Breadalbane and now in the British Museum, tells the story clearly. In essence this is an Irish brooch, its ornament influenced by Pictish, which was made in Ireland and taken to Scotland where a new,

93 The Breadalbane Brooch. Brooches of this type represent the development of the 'Hunterston Brooch' type, and it dates from the late eighth century. The terminals were originally joined, but the joining bar has been cut away, removing in the process a panel of inset filigree. It was probably made by the Scots of Dalriada. It is named after a collector, Lord Breadalbane

94 St John's Cross, Iona. The finest of the series of 'high crosses' to be found in Iona, it represents an offshoot of the tradition of erecting High Crosses in Ireland – Iona maintained close links with Ireland. The details of the ornament can be compared with that in some manuscripts of the seventh to eighth centuries, and it probably should be dated to the later eighth century

165

95 'Face-cross' cross-slab, Riskbuie, Colonsay. This slab depicts the Crucifixion, and belongs to a small group of stones in Ireland and Scotland which date from the end of the seventh and early in the eighth century. Their prototypes are to be found in the eastern Mediterranean, and they attest contacts with this area

Pictish-style pin has been added and the septa joining the terminals have been cut away to give it the true penannular shape the Picts favoured.

In Dalriada itself sculptural developments were to influence Ireland. On the island of Iona that most Irish of monuments, the High Cross, was developed. The antecedents were wooden funerary or preaching crosses, and the first steps towards their translation into stone had taken place in Ireland, where gradually the cross which had adorned flat rectangular slabs was first allowed to modify the shape of the slab then free itself from the surrounding stone. The earliest free-standing stone crosses are perhaps the 'face crosses' of Ireland and Scotland that owe their form to Egyptian 'ankh' crosses, and these may date from the seventh century. What part they played in the development of free-standing crosses is unclear, but what is certain is that on Iona the free-standing cross richly decorated with Celtic ornament was fully evolved by the eighth century.

It was in Pictland, however, that Celtic art reached its greatest pinnacle in Britain. Pictish sculpture is among the finest in Dark Age Europe. It is chiefly remarkable for its complex series of symbols, the meaning of which has eluded generation after generation of antiquaries, and the interpretation of which has led sober scholars to flights of wild fancy. The symbols first appear on rough monolithic pillars of undressed stone and unworked slabs, incised with great economy of line, and with a great feel for the texture of the stone that is being engraved. There are two types, symbols representing a series of naturalistic birds and beasts which were to be found in Pictish hills and valleys, along with two creatures that could never be seen in any zoo, and a series of abstract symbols some of which bear a resemblance to everyday objects available to the Picts, but most of which defy description.

Everything about these symbols is a mystery. On the earliest stones the same form of the symbols appears throughout Pictland, suggesting that they are like pictograms, each symbol having a particular meaning which was understood universally. How old are they? Again the answer is we do not know. It is known that they were still being used as late as the ninth century from their appearance on cross-slabs of that time, and their appearance also on silver objects of the seventh century implies that by that time they were in common use. Comb symbols depict types not in general use much before the fourth century AD, and some of the other symbols might support this conclusion. Another clue might suggest that they were first used on stones in the fourth or early fifth century, at the time when the Picts were becoming a formidable force. The shape of the stones recalls Roman tombstones and the inscribed memorial stones of the fifth and sixth centuries in western Britain. The form of some of the symbols too hints at possible Roman inspiration. One need only compare a Roman altar found at Vindolanda (Chesterholm) on Hadrian's Wall with some Pictish symbols to see a similarity. The symbols may well be the same as those that were worn as tattoos that gave the Picts their Roman name. Some may have been personal badges, others tombstones, and others still might have been boundary markers.

A few of the naturalistic animals that were depicted show marked similarities to evangelist symbols and other beasts that appear in Northumbrian manuscripts and other manifestations of Dark Age art. Whether the creatures that adorn the Book of Durrow and the manuscript Gospel book known as the Corpus Christi 197 are modelled on Pictish representations or vice versa is a chicken-and-egg argument of a type which all too often besets Dark Age studies. While it cannot be disputed that the Pictish renderings are on the whole more competent and display a greater economy of line, both Picts and Northumbrians were probably drawing their inspiration from a common pool of motifs that was being disseminated in Dark Age Europe in the centuries of the Great Migrations.

96 Typical Class I Pictish symbol stone, from Easterton of Roseisle. Perhaps sixth century. The meaning of these symbols is obscure; the stones could have been tombstones or boundary markers

(a) (b)

97 (a) The Aberlemno Churchyard Cross, Angus. One of the finest of the Class II Pictish stones, the back carries more mysterious symbols and a battle scene. Eighth century. (b) The Aberlemno Roadside Cross. This fine Pictish slab, standing 2.82 m high, has mourning angels on either side of the cross. The reverse has symbols and a hunting scene. Some similarities to Anglo-Saxon Mercian sculpture are detectable in this slab. Eighth century

167

98 Pictish cross-slab, Meigle No. 2, Perthshire. This huge stone, 2.46 m high, is a classic example of the 'Boss Style' in Class II Pictish sculpture. Grotesque animals adorn the face. The reverse shows Daniel and a procession of hunters. Late eighth century

99 Pictish arch, Forteviot, Perthshire. Late ninth–tenth century. Post-dating the period of the historical kingdom of the Picts, this shows the continuity of the sculptural tradition. In shape it recalls the single stone arches of Anglo-Saxon churches. It is 1.98 m long

The early symbol stones are the manifestations of an art in its infancy, an art which was to blossom under the influence of Irish and Anglo-Saxon styles into a tradition of maturity and sophistication. Alas, the destruction of manuscripts has meant that we have been deprived of one medium in which the art of the Picts may have been expressed to a great degree of excellence. Only one manuscript survives which is probably of Pictish hand, but that has claims to be the finest to come out of medieval Europe – the Book of Kells. This Gospel book was produced in the eighth century, and taken from Iona off the coast of Dalriada to the monastery of Kells in Co. Westmeath for fear of Viking raids, as a colophon explains. It may have been finished in Ireland, but Irish it most certainly is not. If it was produced in an Iona scriptorium, it was the handiwork of a Pictish monk or possibly a Dalriadan strongly influenced by Pictish taste. Distinctive of the Book of Kells is its wealth of amusing detail – human figures abound, little dumpy figures with large heads and comical faces of a type that is commonplace in later Pictish sculpture but is largely absent in Irish manuscript art. The Kells artist too shows a natural sympathy for animals that is based on prolonged observation. On the Qui Fuit page two rats gnaw on a church wafer observed by two cats, who lazily bide their time. The intricacy of the ornament is unsurpassed: triskeles, spirals, peltas, interlace and a host of other elements are intertwined into patterns of breathtaking complexity. It is possible to study the XRI page for hours without tiring of the intricacies, which in spite of their apparent exuberant confusion were set out from a carefully laid-out plan, the master design of which was traced with compasses before drawing commenced.

The Book of Kells shares the monumentality of its conception with some of the later Pictish cross-slabs, decorated with a wealth of biblical and secular scenes as well as the by now

familiar symbols carved in relief. The most notable are the huge cross-slabs of the so-called 'Boss Style', and the contemporary products of the Meigle School in Angus. Some stand 2.4 m high and are correspondingly broad, and in their monumentality are unmatched in contemporary sculpture.

In metalworking, too, the Picts excelled. Even here the Pictish love of animal ornament and figural work is apparent. A bronze pin, found in 1974 at Golspie in Sutherland, is surmounted by a comical human mask, its brow furrowed as though contemplating some insoluble problem. Snub-nosed animals, confronted as on penannular brooches, stare at each other on a variety of small bronzes.

The ultimate achievement of Pictish metalworking, however, lay in silverwork. A foretaste of the achievements that were to come is provided by the massive silver chains, some with terminal rings decorated with Pictish symbols, that have been found mainly in the south of Scotland where they were no doubt left by Pictish raiding parties. Weighing up to 2.6 kg each, they show enormous technical skill in their fabrication – a special tool had to be made to copy one from a hoard from Gaulcross, Banff. Accomplished too, is the silverwork from the hoard found at Norrie's Law, Fife, with its huge plain silver brooches, and its plates decorated with neatly executed symbols, which may have been Pictish versions of the 'phalerae' or insignia worn by Roman soldiers. It was from Roman tables that most of the silver used by the Picts came – a Roman spoon, crushed for remelting, came from Norrie's Law – and in the vast hoard of Roman silverware found at Traprain Law in 1919 we can

100 A worried Pict adorns this stick-pin of bronze from Golspie, Sutherland, found in a garden in 1974. The surviving part of the pin is 55 mm long. It shows Pictish skill in minor metalworking. Probably late eighth century

101 (*Left*) The Monymusk Reliquary, or Brecbennoch of St Columba. It was made to contain a relic of St Columba, and was supposedly carried into battle at Bannockburn. A mere 10 cm long, it is carved out of a block of wood and covered with bronze plates. The front is faced with engraved silver, and bears Pictish-style animals, suggesting it was made in Pictland. The ornamental roundels are decorated with chip-carved interlace, and the hinges are enamelled with red and yellow, displaying a triskele. *c.*AD 700

102 The Norrie's Law hoard, Fife. This hoard is of crucial importance in the dating of Pictish metalwork and the Pictish symbols. The penannular objects are akin to brooches of the type represented in Plate 89, but are not exactly like any other brooches, and may have been used for some other purpose. The 'phalerae' are decorated with Pictish symbols, and may have been for horse harness. The silver repoussé plate has trumpet-pattern spirals, and recalls some earlier Iron Age objects such as the Irish Monasterevin discs and the 'Caledonian' armlets of the second century in Scotland. The hoard is dated on the supposed association of a Byzantine coin of the late sixth century

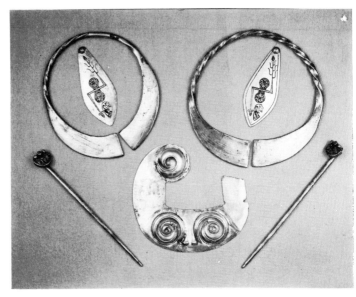

103 Pictish brooch, reputedly found near Perth and purchased in a Perth antique shop in the 1880s. Diameter: 7 cm. Pictish features include the 'cusps' joining the terminals to the hoop, the curved-ended panel on the hoop and the treatment of the terminals. Gilt silver, eighth century, or early ninth. Note the relief-modelled heads on the terminals

170

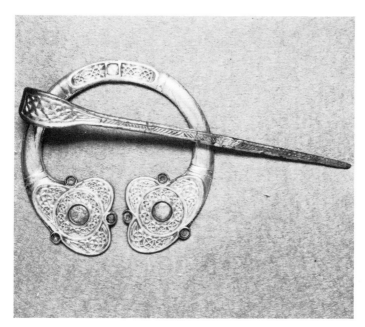

104 One of the so-called 'Cadboll' brooches, from Rogart, Sutherland, of gilt silver. Of the same family of brooches as those from the St Ninian's Isle Treasure, and datable to around AD 800. Diameter: 6 cm

probably see a hoard of loot carried off by Pictish raiders pillaging the south for the raw material for their own products.

Pictish silverwork was at its finest in the eighth century, at the time when the St Ninian's Isle Treasure was being made. The St Ninian's Isle Treasure, however, does not stand alone. Every bit as competent is the pair of silver gilt brooches found at Perth in the 1880s, one inset with gold filigree and amber and ornamented on the terminals with animal heads modelled in relief – the same device of relief-modelled birds' heads can be seen employed on the silver gilt 'Cadboll' brooch from Rogart, Sutherland, executed in the St Ninian's Isle tradition and dating from around the beginning of the ninth century. In these brooches can be seen Celtic craftsmanship at its very best, rich in its ornament but at the same time showing the restraint absent in Irish work.

Epilogue:
Celtic Twilight

When Henry 2, King of England, had learned from the songs of
the British bards that Arthur the most noble heroe of the Britains,
whose courage had so often shattered the Saxons, was bury'd at
Glassenbury between two Pyramids, he order'd search to be
made for the body: and they had scarse digged seven foot deep,
but they light upon a cross'd stone, or a stone in the back part
whereof was fasten'd a rude leaden *Cross*, something broad. This
being pull'd out, appear'd to have an Inscription upon it: and
under it, almost nine foot deep, they found a Coffin made of
hollow'd oak, wherein were reposited the bones of the famous
Arthur. As to the Inscription, which being taken from the original
was formerly writ in the monastery of Glassenbury, I thought it
proper to give a draught of it because of the Antinquity of it's
letters. The letters have a sort of barbarous and Gothick
appearance and are plain evidence of the barbarity of the age,
which was so involv'd in a fatal sort of mist, that no-one was
found to celebrate the name of K. Arthur.

In these words William Camden, the great sixteenth-
century antiquary, described the discovery of the tomb of
King Arthur at Glastonbury, Somerset, nearly four
centuries before. In legend the greatest of the Dark Age
Celts lives on into the Middle Ages and the present day. It is
not surprising that the Dark Ages, that period of Celtic
turmoil and chaos, should have given rise to one of the most
famous legends in Britain.

The growth of the myth of Arthur has been easier to
reconstruct than the historical fact. By the late sixth or
seventh century Arthur was beginning to be a popular
personal name – it is unknown before the time of the
historical Arthur and its sudden popularity simply takes its
social place as an early form of the trend that leads to a spate
of young Winstons or Elvises.

By the ninth century Arthur had assumed more obvious
heroic status. In the Gododdin poem, composed in the sixth
century and describing a heroic but futile campaign in
northern Britain, a hero called Gwawrddur is extolled thus:

> He glutted black ravens on the fort wall
> Though he was not Arthur.

The couplet was probably inserted when the poem was put
down in writing in the ninth century, at a time when all

manner of wonders were being associated with Arthur's name. The time was nearing when Arthur would have to live again.

The arena moves to Glastonbury, the traditional site of Arthur's grave. Had Arthur been buried with the type of memorial stone that was current in the sixth century, it might have been inscribed

HIC IACIT ARTURIUS SEPULTUS IN HOC TUMULO

It has been suggested that such a memorial stone erected over the grave of Arthur was still standing in the tenth century when St Dunstan was abbot of Glastonbury. Dunstan carried out various building operations at Glaston-bury, and one of them involved enclosing the old cemetery with a stone wall and raising the area with a clay bank, which was laid on top of a mausoleum, demolished perhaps just before. This mausoleum certainly contained the grave of an important personage – could it have been that of Arthur, buried after Camlann? If so, Dunstan would have moved the remains and reburied them with a suitable memorial in a more convenient place. When Arthur's grave came to be opened in the twelfth century a lead cross was found, in circumstances which we have already heard described in the words of William Camden at the opening of the chapter. Camden drew it before it was lost. The lettering is in keeping with that current in the tenth century, and if, as some have suggested, the cross was made by the Glastonbury monks in the twelfth century, then it must be explained as a deliberate forgery, copying old lettering which they supposed might be mistaken for that of the sixth century. Such a forgery is not impossible, but it is inherently more likely that the cross was made on the order of Dunstan when the remains were moved from the mausoleum, and followed roughly the original formula, the inscription recorded by Camden being

HIC IACET SEPULTUS INCLITUS REX ARTURIUS
IN INSULA AVALONIA
'Here lies buried the famous king Arthur in the Isle of Avalon'

This attempt at following the original might explain the sixth-century character of a few of the letters, noted by some commentators.

Politics now complicate the saga. In the early twelfth century the Normans were still relative newcomers in England, anxious to prove their claim to rule. One thing they were not, and that was Anglo-Saxons, and therefore claims to Saxon forebears would have sounded lame in the extreme. On the other hand, comparisons between the

Normans and British heroes sounded more promising. For this a suitable hero had to be found to fit the bill. The kings of France had their own great hero, Charlemagne, and round him and his legendary knight Roland a whole cycle of myth had been built up that came to be known as the Matter of France. The story of Aeneas provided another traditional cycle in Europe, the Matter of Rome, but neither of these had any real relevance to the national spirit the Normans were trying to drum up at the time of the troubles between

105 Folio 94 from the British Museum MS Add. 10294, a fourteenth-century version of *Le Roman de Lancelot du Lac et de la Mort du Roi Artu*. It shows the mortally wounded king Arthur sitting at the edge of the lake while Sir Bedevere casts his sword, Excalibur, back into the waters, where a hand rises to take it. This is how the Middle Ages saw Arthur

Stephen and Matilda. What was needed was Arthur. Like the Normans, he fought the Saxons, and like the Normans, he won.

Had it not been for a curious chance, however, Arthur might never have been resurrected. It just so happened that the librarian of Malmesbury Abbey, William, learnt of the story of Arthur while visiting his fellow Benedictines at Glastonbury. William of Malmesbury, who was a stickler for truth, did not get very far in his investigation of the Arthur case, but through him word of Arthur reached his patron, the Earl of Gloucester. Soon the story reached his contemporary, the best-selling writer Geoffrey of Monmouth, who provided in his *History of the Kings of Britain* not only the facts but a good deal else beside. Geoffrey's book reached its climax with the career of Arthur, and almost overnight Geoffrey's fiction became England's fact. In 1187 Henry II called his grandson Arthur, in the hope that he would become Arthur II of England.

The Welsh, not unnaturally, were outraged that their hero should suddenly be adopted by the Norman English. It looked as though Henry II had overstepped his mark, and an ugly scene was going to follow. But trouble was averted by cunning stratagem. Had not Henry been told by an ancient bard in Wales that Arthur was not still alive (as many claimed), but dead and buried? If his grave were found the dispute would be settled, depending on whether it lay in England or Wales. Suddenly it was 'discovered' that Arthur's grave was at Glastonbury. Henry wanted a thorough search for the tomb, but the matter was delayed until 1190. In that year the abbey was conveniently burnt down, and after the holocaust, in the clearing up, lo and behold, there was Arthur's tomb. We have heard the circumstances of the discovery of the coffin in Camden's words. When the coffin was opened, inside lay the skeleton of a tall man, his skull damaged. Alongside were the bones of a smaller person, and a lock of golden hair, which fell to pieces when picked up by a monk. Here was Arthur, and beside him Guinevere. There is no doubt that the Glastonbury monks found something they believed to be the grave of Arthur – the site of their discovery came to light in excavation in 1962. He was reburied in a more fitting casket, and there, it might seem, the story ends.

Alas for Arthur, his peace was to be rudely disturbed again, once more for political objectives. Edward I was fighting Wales, and it was deemed psychologically important to show that Arthur was not still alive in the land of the Cymru but dead and buried in England. It was determined to recover the bones and in the presence of Edward I to translate them to a more regal resting place (which, incidentally, survived until the Reformation). The event was described by Adam of Domerham in these words (quoted in Geoffrey Ashe, *The Quest for Arthur's Britain*, London, 1972, p. 99):

> The lord Edward . . . with his consort, the lady Eleanor, came to Glastonbury to celebrate Easter . . . the following Tuesday. . . at dusk, the lord king had the tomb of the famous king Arthur opened. Wherein in two caskets painted with their pictures and arms, were found separately the bones of the said king, and those of Queen Guinevere, which were of marvellous beauty. . . . On the following day . . . the lord king replaced the bones of the king and the queen those of the queen, each in their own casket, having wrapped them in costly silks. When they had been sealed they ordered the tomb to be placed forthwith in front of the high altar, after the removal of the skulls for the veneration of the people.

Such was the fate of the mortal remains of Arthur. The rest of the story belongs to medieval romance. The tale was

175

taken up and elaborated, embroidered with medieval ideas of chivalry, of courtly manners and of love. New tales were grafted on to the old, and minstrels in both France and Britain told them wherever they went. Chrétien de Troyes was one of the first, Malory was the greatest, coming at the end of an age and crystallizing the whole into a coherent saga which was called *Morte d'Arthur*. Arthur may have lived, but had he been able to read Malory, he would have failed to recognize his world in any line.

> Sir, said Sir Bedevere, what man is there interred that ye pray so fast for? Fair son, said the hermit, I wot not verily, but by deeming. But this night, at midnight, here came a number of ladies, and brought hither a dead corpse, and prayed me to bury him; and here they offered me an hundred tapers, and gave me an hundred besants. Alas, said Sir Bedevere, that was my lord King Arthur, that lieth buried in this chapel! . . . Thus of Arthur I find never more written in books than he authorized, nor more of the certainty of his death I never heard tell, but thus was he led away in a ship wherein were three queens: that one was King Arthur's sister queen Morgan le Fay: the other was the queen of Northgalis: the third was the queen of the Wester Lands.

Here is the end of the whole story of king Arthur and with it the Celts live on into the present day. Without a doubt the most enduring legacy that the Celts left came from the mists of antiquity a thousand years before king Arthur; place-names. Celts who walked the island nearly three thousand years ago are commemorated on numerous signposts, maps, guidebooks, the names of cafés, bookstalls and pubs. The areas extensively settled by the Anglo-Saxons have widespread Germanic names, others have exotic-sounding names from the period of the Normans or the Crusades. Very few have even partly Roman names, since the Romans merely Latinized Celtic words. Hundreds all over the country, increasing in density towards the west, are derived almost directly from the names used by king Arthur, or king Cunobelin, queen Boudicca or the high king Divitiacus. The list of famous places of Celtic origin is impressive – London (the town of Londinos), Dover (water), Kent, Manchester, Cirencester. The Thames, Severn, Humber, Tyne and Tees are just a few of the rivers with a Celtic ancestry to their names. In Wales the original names have hardly been changed, merely modified as the language itself evolved. The place-names of Scotland derive from a less ancient past – most are Gaelic in origin with some Pictish and some Scandinavian. Nevertheless these are Celtic and a distribution map of the main elements in place-names shows a very large proportion owing their existence to the Celtic peoples of the past.

Literature is probably the second most important carrier of the Celtic heritage. We might read the excerpt from the scythed chariot (p. 22) with total astonishment if we were not familiar with more modern writing in closely similar style. Dylan Thomas, Samuel Beckett, and the Scottish poet D. M. Black, for instance, all achieve some aspects common to more ancient bards. The true Celtic poet draws his parallels from unlikely sources, they are surreal but no less intensely vivid. This is the bardic tradition that stems from the public recitation before the chief and his followers in the great hall. It is something barbarian and recurs in the literature of other societies with a strong barbarian past. This heritage is something apart from the conscious antiquarianism in some modern Welsh poetry, or the pseudo-Celticism of Yeats's Celtic Twilight movement. This was a literary equivalent to pre-Raphaelitism in which a group of nineteenth-century poets tried to create a new Celtic literature without any real understanding of the original. For them Celtic literature was romantic, full of tragic love affairs, fairy people, magical twilit worlds and beautiful immortals. Their creations were far removed from any Celtic original. Celtic survival in literature shows itself in a completely modern guise in the style of expression rather than the ideas it expresses.

By the same token the 'Celtic art' sold today in craft shops is not a survival of tradition. The history of Celtic art from the Middle Ages is curious. In the western Highlands of Scotland the tradition was kept alive quite strongly in sculpture, an important focus being the island of Iona. In the western Highlands grave-slabs can be seen which display both a continuation of the old styles of interlace and new elements derived from contemporary medieval art. To a lesser extent, sculptural traditions persisted well into the Middle Ages in Wales, though once more watered down for medieval taste. The sixteenth century saw a new Celtic art in Scotland and Ireland. To what extent this owed anything to tradition and to what extent it was prompted by geometric interlace patterns that were making their appearance again on imports from Renaissance Italy is a debatable point. It is probably fair to say that, long familiar with interlace patterns from the sculptures that could still be seen in the countryside, Celtic artists took to the new motifs readily, and began to employ them in the decoration of various objects. Take, for instance, the Eglinton Casket, now in the National Museum of Antiquities, Edinburgh, with its ivory panels of intricate interlace. Its shape betrays it as an object of the sixteenth century, but its ornament is so close to that of the

106 The Eglinton Casket. There was a rival of the use of interlace ornament in Scotland and Ireland in the sixteenth century, perhaps fostered by Italianate taste at the time. This object, often ascribed to the Dark Ages, is probably a sixteenth-century product of the west Highlands

107 Powder horn dated 1693. Interlace again adorns this typical product of a Scottish Highland workshop – it was probably made in the north-east

Dark Ages that it has more than once been claimed as a tenth-century work. This 'new Celtic art', if it can so be called, persisted during the seventeenth century (when complex interlace was used to ornament powder horns) and into the eighteenth century. The tradition petered out for a short time, but Queen Victoria's tour of the Highlands and her interest with all things Scottish brought about a Celtic revival. This time craftsmen turned their attentions to imitating old designs, rather than the creation of new. On some objects old patterns were copied, while others used famous works as a starting point for totally new interpretations. Compare the brooch illustrated with the Hunterston Brooch that it imitates. The animal ornament has been replaced with foliage scrolls of the type beloved of the Victorians, and giant polished pebbles and citrines are a travesty of the delicate inlays on the original. Such 'Celtic' jewellery is still made today, all too often inspired by Norse rather than Celtic imagery. It is not a traditional craft but a conscious revival, geared entirely to a tourist market.

By looking at art and literature, then, it is possible to say

The Victorian taste for all things Scottish, fostered by Sir Walter Scott and later Queen Victoria, led to a spate of 'Celtic crafts' which have been produced ever since. This brooch is modelled on the Hunterston brooch (Plate 90) but bears little real resemblance to it

that something of the Celtic traditions survived the Middle Ages, though much of what is claimed as 'Celtic' is a deliberate imitation inspired by an imperfect understanding of the original. This of course extends to other 'Celtic' traditions. The Welsh National Eisteddfod is a creation of the nineteenth century, and the 'druids' who preside are an antiquarian's fancy, as far removed from historical accuracy as the cartoonist's dinosaur-hunting caveman; the druid presiding over the 1977 Eisteddfod at Wrexham wore as his insignia a copy of a Bronze Age gold necklet, which had been fashioned centuries before there were druids. Not only does it belong to another age, but to another land, for it is a replica of an Irish object, the like of which has never been found in Welsh soil. Before we smile at this image of the Celtic past, we could do worse than look at another, provided by the Scottish painter William Hole (1845–1917), to be found adorning the wall of the National Portrait Gallery in Edinburgh. Here depicted is the conversion of Bridei of the Picts by the Irish cleric Columba. The gentle saint has become a symbol of the missionary spirit of the nineteenth

109 The Victorian vision of the Celtic past is epitomised by this wall painting in the Scottish National Portrait Gallery (the same building as the National Museum of Antiquities of Scotland). Painted by William Hole (1846–1917), it depicts the Mission of St Columba to the Picts. The Picts are in possession of an assortment of antiquities, mostly Bronze Age and not all British

century. He is a Victorian, preaching to a group of African villagers his own brand of uncompromising faith. Bridei is broody, but behind him stands his wife, a Victorian matriarch, unwilling to take any nonsense from either her husband or Columba. Bridei wears an armlet of Caledonian type made perhaps in the second century; his cloak is fastened by the eighth-century Hunterston Brooch, or a version of it, he wears a helmet of a type fashionable among the Villanovans of Italy in the Iron Age, perhaps in the eighth century BC, and he sits on a block carved with ninth-century interlace. Across his knees lies his sword. The scabbard is perhaps Iron Age English, the sword hilt itself looks more medieval. In the foreground sits a warrior with a Bronze Age shield; he and another warrior carry spears of different Bronze Age dates. One of Columba's followers carries a type of crozier fashionable in Ireland around AD 1100, and all are set in a rocky scene taken straight from an eighteenth-century antiquary's druid scrapbook. Yet, at first glance, there is nothing in this picture that jars on the eye. It evokes to the twentieth-century mind almost as faithful an image of the Celt as he is thought of as it did for the nineteenth-century. So tied up with our own imagery are we that the Celts continue to elude us. They are there and they are not there, like a mask in an Iron Age bronze. Each generation sees in the pattern what it wants, and moves on. The Celts' contribution to Western society lies not in what they achieved, but in the myths to which they gave rise.

Epilogue:
Celtic Twilight

The Best of Celtic Britain

This gazetteer lists fifty of the very best visible remains of the Celts in Britain, arranged geographically.

Site	County	OS Grid Ref	Description
Chysauster	Cornwall	SW473350	Iron Age village of stone huts
Carn Euny	Cornwall	SW 142283	Similar village, with *fogou*
Tintagel	Cornwall	SX 049891	Dark Age settlement or monastery
Hembury	Devon	ST 112030	Iron Age hillfort
Maiden Castle	Dorset	SY 669885	Finest Iron Age hillfort in Britain
Hod Hill	Dorset	ST 856106	Iron Age hillfort, with Roman fort inside it
Hambledon Hill	Dorset	ST 845126	Iron Age hillfort
Badbury Ring	Somerset	ST 964030	Iron Age hillfort
South Cadbury	Somerset	ST 618246	Major Iron Age hillfort with Dark Age occupation
Ham Hill	Somerset	ST 479168	Iron Age hillfort
Wansdyke	Wilts	SU 050660	Linear earthwork, Dark Age
Scratchbury	Wilts	ST 911443	Iron Age hillfort
Yarnbury	Wilts	SU 035404	Iron Age hillfort
Beacon Hill	Hants	SU 457572	Iron Age hillfort
Ladle Hill	Hants	SU 478568	Unfinished Iron Age fort
Danebury	Hants	SU 323377	Iron Age hillfort
Quarley Hill	Hants	SU 262423	Iron Age hillfort
Liddington Castle	Berks	SU 208796	Iron Age fort, with Dark Age occupation
Uffington Castle	Berks	SU 299863	Iron Age hillfort and White Horse
Hollingbury	Sussex	TQ 322078	Iron Age hillfort
Mount Caburn	Sussex	TQ 444089	Iron Age hillfort
Trundle	Sussex	SU 877111	Iron Age hillfort
Cissbury	Sussex	TQ 139080	Iron Age hillfort
Chanctonbury	Sussex	TQ 139121	Iron Age hillfort
Bredon Hill	Glos	SO 957402	Iron Age hillfort
Uley Bury	Glos	ST 785989	Iron Age hillfort
Croft Ambrey	Hereford	SO 444668	Iron Age hillfort
Old Oswestry	Shropshire	SJ 295304	Iron Age hillfort
Almondbury	Yorks	SE 153141	Iron Age hillfort
Ingleborough	Yorks	SD 742746	Iron Age hillfort
Tre'er Ceiri	Gwynedd	SH 374447	Iron Age hillfort
Din Lligwy	Anglesey	SH 496862	Stone hut group, Iron Age
Margam	Glamorgan	SS 802862	Collection of Dark Age sculptured stones

Site	County	OS Grid Ref	Description
Carew	Pembs	SN 046036	Free-standing Dark Age cross
Aberlemno	Angus	NO 522557	Pictish sculptured stones
Finavon	Angus	NO 506556	Iron Age vitrified fort
St Vigeans	Angus	NO 639429	Collection of Pictish sculpture
The Caterthuns	Angus	NO 555668 and NO 548660	Two adjacent hillforts, Iron Age
Meigle	Perths	NN 287446	Collection of Pictish sculptures
Sueno's Stone	Moray	NJ 047595	Richly decorated late Pictish slab
Dunadd	Argyll	NR 837936	Dark Age fort
Iona	Argyll	NM 284243	Monastic site
Dun Carloway	Lewis	NB 190413	Iron Age broch
Glenelg	Inverness	NG 829172 and NG 834172	Iron Age brochs, Dun Telve and Dun Troddan
Dundornadilla	Sutherland	NH 455449	Iron Age broch
Aikerness	Orkney	HY 383268	Iron Age broch and post-broch settlement
Midhowe	Orkney	HY 371308	Iron Age broch and post-broch settlement
Mousa	Shetland	HU 457237	Finest broch in Britain
Clickhimin	Shetland	HU 464408	Multi-phase Iron Age settlement with broch
Jarlshof	Shetland	HU 398096	Multi-phase Iron Age settlement, with broch and wheelhouses

Further Reading

General

Many books have been written about the Celts, many of them perpetuating old myths rather than clarifying them. Although very inadequate in its treatment of the archaeological evidence, M. Dillon and N. Chadwick, *The Celtic Realms* (2nd edn, London, 1972) is one of the best, and is particularly illuminating on literature and secular institutions. For the prehistoric background of the Continental Celts, although again out of date, S. Piggott, *Ancient Europe* (Edinburgh, 1965) and S. Piggott and G. Clark, *Prehistoric Societies* (London, 1965) are the best introductions. The best book on the Continental Celts from an archaeological standpoint is J. Filip, *Celtic Civilization and its Heritage* (Prague, 1962), though its comments on Britain are very outdated and inaccurate. More reliable, but again not very detailed in its treatment of archaeology, is T. G. E. Powell, *The Celts* (London, 1958) which is well illustrated. J. Raftery (ed.), *The Celts* (Cork, 1964), is a useful paperback and very readable – it was originally a series of radio broadcasts.

Iron Age

The reader is very fortunate in now having two excellent texts on the archaeology of Iron Age Britain. B. W. Cunliffe, *Iron Age Communities in Britain* (2nd edn, London, 1978) is the most exhaustive, since it covers the whole of Britain and all aspects of archaeology. D. W. Harding, *The Iron Age in Lowland Britain* (London, 1974) is geographically more restricted and tends to concentrate on particular topics – it is, however, easier to read.

Celtic art is dealt with in a series of books. The standard work on Continental Celtic art is P. Jacobsthal, *Early Celtic Art* (2 vols, Oxford, 1944), and its companion study on British Celtic art, P. Jacobsthal and E. M. Jope, *Early Celtic Art in Britain* (Oxford, 1977). J. V. S. Megaw, *Art of the European Iron Age* (Bath, 1972), provides a series of plates of British and Contintental art with excellent notes and introduction. A similar series of notes on particular pieces can be found in S. Piggott, *Early Celtic Art* (Edinburgh, 1970, Arts Council Exhibition catalogue). The standard historical survey of Celtic art in Britain is C. Fox, *Pattern and Purpose* (Cardiff, 1958), though some of Fox's 'Schools' are not now generally maintained. For Brigantian and other northern art, M. Macgregor, *Early Celtic Art in North Britain* (Leicester, 1976) is a fundamental source. From a wider standpoint, T. G. E. Powell, *Prehistoric Art* (London, 1966) sets Celtic art in its European context. I. Finlay's *Celtic Art* (London, 1973) deals with not just prehistoric but with Dark Age Celtic art, and is therefore quite a useful introduction.

Celtic religion is well served by A. Ross, *Pagan Celtic Britain* (London, 1967), which deals with Romano-British as well as Iron Age Celtic cults. S. Piggott, *The Druids* (London, 1968) is the best modern survey of that subject, though T. Kendrick, *The Druids: A Study in Celtic Prehistory* (London, 1927, and New York, 1966) remains a classic.

Celtic society is dealt with in M. Dillon, *Early Irish Society* (Dublin, 1954, and later reprints), which again being a series of radio talks is very readable. So too is K. H. Jackson, *The Oldest Irish Tradition: a Window on the Iron Age* (Cambridge, 1964), which was a lecture on Irish literature as a key to Iron Age society.

Of the more specialist literature, three collections of studies of regional Iron Age problems are all useful. All are papers given to conferences organized by the Council for British Archaeology. They are: S. Frere, *Problems of the Iron Age in Southern Britain* (London, 1961), A. L. F. Rivet (ed.), *The Iron Age in Northern Britain* (Edinburgh, 1966) and A. C. Thomas (ed.), *The Iron Age in the Irish Sea Province* (London, 1972). Collections of papers on hillforts and their problems are to be found in M. Jesson and D. Hill (eds), *The Iron Age and its Hill-forts* (Southampton, 1971) and D. W. Harding (ed.), *Hillforts; a Survey of Research in Britain and Ireland* (London, 1977). Oppida, both British and Continental, are dealt with in B. W. Cunliffe and T. Rowley *Oppida in Barbarian Europe* (Oxford, 1976).

Of individual short studies, one is worth singling out. This is B. W. Cunliffe and T. Rowley, *Oppida in Barbarian Europe* (Oxford, *a New Outline* (London, 1974), pp. 233–62, which can be read in conjunction with the preceding article on the Bronze Age by C. Burgess.

The Roman Iron Age

Books on the Roman Iron Age have not been written. The north, however, is dealt with in the now old-fashioned I. A. Richmond, *Roman and Native in North Britain* (London, 1958), and various problems are dealt with in A. C. Thomas (ed.), *Rural Settlement in Roman Britain* (London, 1966). For the Roman period generally the standard survey is S. Frere, *Britannia* (London, 1964).

Post-Roman

Only one general survey covers the whole period and the whole of Britain from an archaeological standpoint: L. Laing, *The Archaeology of Late Celtic Britain and Ireland, c.400–1200 AD* (London, 1975). For the period down to AD 634, however, L. Alcock, *Arthur's Britain* (London, 1971) is first-rate, and deals with Saxons as well as Celts. For a detailed study of the history of this period, J. Morris, *The Age of Arthur* (London, 1973) is very stimulating, though alas extremely unreliable in places in its interpretation. Its eccentricities, however, should not be allowed to discourage people from reading it. More reliable historically, but not otherwise, is N. K. Chadwick's *Celtic Britain* (London, 1963). For the history of Scotland in the period the best survey is still H. M. Chadwick, *Early Scotland* (Cambridge, 1949), while for Wales the best survey is still J. Lloyd, *A History of Wales* (London, 1939).

On particular topics, the Picts are covered in F. T. Wainwright, *The Problem of the Picts* (London, 1955) and in I. Henderson, *The Picts* (London, 1964), which is lavishly illustrated, and has a particularly useful survey of Pictish history.

A charming introduction to the Church in Celtic lands is provided by N. K. Chadwick, *The Age of the Saints in the Early Celtic Church* (2nd edn, Oxford, 1963), while the archaeology of the Church is dealt with more prosaically by A. C. Thomas, *The Early Christian Archaeology of North Britain* (Oxford, 1971).

Those interested in Arthurian problems should read G. Ashe (ed.), *The Quest for Arthur's Britain* (London, 1968), and they will also find L. Alcock, *'By South Cadbury is that Camelot . . .'* (London, 1972), which is an account of his excavations on the site of South Cadbury, fascinating reading.

Celtic survival

There are no books on the Celts after the arrival of the Normans in Celtic lands. L. Laing (ed.), *Studies in Celtic Survival* (Oxford, 1977), may, however, be found useful as a collection of studies on various regions and topics.

Index